Talking With Your Child

![DP] The Danbury Press

WOMAN ALIVE

Talking With Your Child

by Mary Hands

Inter
i
bérica, S.A. de Ediciones

Series Coordinator: John Mason
Design Director: Guenther Radtke
Picture Editor: Peter Cook
Copy Editor: Mitzi Bales
Research: Elizabeth Lake
Sarah Waters
Consultants: Beppie Harrison
Jo Sandilands

Contents

Talking with your child ought to be the easiest thing in the world, but often isn't – and the reason is that there is a communications gap between parents and their children. This book tries to give helpful guidelines for keeping lines of communication open from crib to college. Stressing the importance of honesty and mutual respect at all stages in parent-child relationships, the author shows how generation gaps can be bridged before – and after – they occur. She also discusses the importance of nonverbal communication, and ways in which parents can help their youngsters to resist harmful group pressures. A final section answers often asked questions on topics such as childhood fears, family arguments, and teenage attitudes to sexual behavior and drugs.

The Unchanging Child

A child of antiquity, a child of today—down through the ages there has been a link in the inner world of children. Childhood has always meant wonder, innocence, and joy.

Below: the beaming face of a healthy and lovable child is like a ray of sunshine, brightening life for himself and for others.

Right: childhood is not always totally free of responsibilities. This Roman mosaic shows a young child in charge of some ducks.

Above: the rough-and-tumble play among these young dandies of 500 years ago bears a close resemblance to boys at fun today.

Right: children make their own fun—and they can find fun in anything. These children of Victorian days are making a game of waving to people on the trains that go by.

6

Above right: only the face is that of a little girl. Otherwise she's dressed exactly like an adult, as 18th-century children were.

Below: isn't it fun to sprinkle the lawn and explain how it's done to kitty? Most tots seem especially to enjoy playing with water.

7

Mother and Child

Does anything evoke more tenderness, more gentle sentimentality than mother and child together? The woman and her offspring have a touching and complete closeness that symbolizes all the ideals of mother love.

Below: the traditional view of the Madonna and Child—placid and saintly—as painted by a Flemish artist about 500 years ago.

Right: alike as sisters, alike as mothers—this painting of Tudor days shows twins who even had their babies at the same time.

Above: this 17th-century painting catches a look that's close to holiness in this mother who gazes fondly at her newborn baby.

Right: protectively strapped to mother's back, baby goes where she goes. This is how mothers carry infants in the Cameroons.

Above: a mother and child of long-ago Colonial America seem warm and loving.

Below: today, as ever, the relationship of mother and child is the highest form of love.

A Child Learns

A child first learns exclusively from his or her parents, and such learning can be a happy shared experience for mother, father, and children. If it is, it can breed a love of knowledge that lasts a whole lifetime.

Right: teaching a child to walk with a four-sided support on wheels is coming back in fashion. This detail of a 17th-century painting shows how it was done back then.

Left: in the days before public education, those who could afford it paid governesses for individual, private teaching at home.

Below: this young lad hasn't yet learned his lesson about being late, and he's fearful of what the schoolmaster will do to him.

Above: this boy of New Guinea is learning how to hunt from an adult of his tribe.

Below: a Saharan Tuareg teaches a little boy his lessons from the Moslem holy book.

Right: learning is more fun than work when a child can read his book with mother.

In an Adult World

Sometimes a child is so talented, or so intelligent that he seems to be an adult in all but age. Sometimes it is circumstance—such as royal birth or parental ambition—that forces a child early into the adult world.

Right: the attitude that children are just little adults comes through in this 18th-century picture of a noble Venetian family.

Below: at the age of 11, Wolfgang Amadeus Mozart had already been a famous concert pianist for four years. He started to compose music at the age of five.

Below right: Albrecht Dürer fulfilled his early promise as a great artist. This self-portrait was done at the age of 13 years.

Above: although this Indian child was enthroned, his adult advisor actually ruled.

Left: one of the most famous child stars of all time, Shirley Temple made her singing and dancing debut in movies at age three.

Above: a champion in the field of sports, Shane Gould of Australia was only 15 when she won five gold medals at the Olympics.

The Child's World

It's the land of make-believe, where games and activities owe a lot to imagination. It's a place for dolls, for pets, for paints and paper and crayons. It's a child's wonderful world.

Right: the spontaneous behavior of a small girl is caught in this otherwise formal portrait of the 1700's. Father looks at the artist, but daughter wants him to see dolly.

Below: lucky children! Not only do they get to dress up fancifully as pretend royalty of the Orient, but they also get painted all decked out in their exotic clothes.

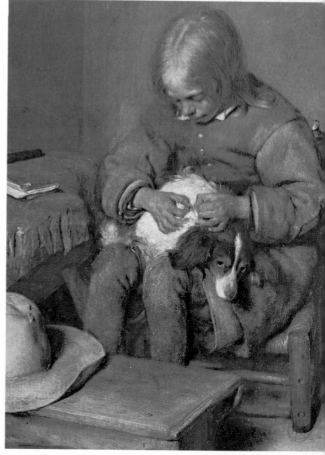

Above: a boy and his dog, then as now, evokes a familiar picture of childhood. This scene was painted in Holland in the 1600's.

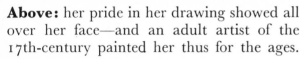

Above: her pride in her drawing showed all over her face—and an adult artist of the 17th-century painted her thus for the ages.

Above: it might be only a toy engine, but it can be as real as real to young children.

Below: the fascination of putting bright colors on paper begins early, as these toddlers intent at drawing with their crayons show.

Getting Through to Each Other

1

From the very first moment that your baby is born, the love you express will get through to him. Love is the most important form of communication in the earliest years— and it's a language anyone can speak and understand.

Talking with your child sounds like the easiest thing in the world, so why should it sometimes prove so difficult? Why do so many parents—and children—complain that a communication gap has opened up between them? How does such a gap come about? How can it be bridged? Most importantly, need such a breakdown in communication ever happen at all?

To answer all these questions, we need to know something about the process of communication itself. We all know, for example, that we communicate by talking, but how much thought do we give to that other half of the communication circuit: listening? This, according to some experts, is even more important to good communication than talking, especially with children.

Think for a moment of those times when you have launched into a favorite topic of conversation with a friend, only to realize that she is no longer listening. Whether your reaction is one of hurt, anger, or frustration, one thing is certain. You no longer feel much like talking. That person has cut you off as effectively as if she had flipped an electric switch. Yet, how often do we do the very same thing to our own children?

One cause of the communication gap between parents and children, some experts say, is the fact that many loving and devoted parents are simply too busy, too caught up in the hundred-and-one preoccupations of their daily lives, to spare time for genuine two-way conversation with their children. While Tommy tells us an excited story over breakfast, we may be busy thinking, "I must remember to take those chops out of the freezer for tonight's dinner," or "That shirt of his is grubby already. I really must get down to some washing," not to mention sneaking a quick look at the clock to see just how much time there is to get it all done. Tommy is quick to sense that mother's thoughts are elsewhere, and either his story peters to a halt, or he devises more dramatic ways to capture her attention.

That doesn't mean that we have to be attentive to our children all the time. With the best will in the world, that would be impossible. Parents are busy people, with hectic schedules to get through every day. But a child needs to be able to count on our full attention some of the time if he is to be convinced that we find his views worth hearing, and love him enough to want to listen to what he has to say. Pretending to listen, however, can be worse than not listening at all. If you really have too many other demands on your time at a particular moment, or you are too tired or worried to listen attentively, it is probably best to say so. There is still a world of difference between saying, "Go away, I'm busy," and "I wish I had time to hear all about it, but you'll be late for school if we don't leave now. When you come home, I promise we'll have a nice, long talk together."

Listening, however, doesn't stop at hearing your child's words. When children talk, they seek—like adults—to share feelings in the hope not just of being heard, but also of being understood. Supposing, for example, that your mother is ill, and you confide to a neighbor how anxious you are. If she replies with a jaunty, "Don't worry; she's bound to be all right," you hardly feel comforted. How differently you might react if she should say a warm, "I'm so sorry. How worried you must be." Her words, her tone of voice tell you she is concerned, and that she appreciates how you are feeling. By her understanding attitude, she encourages you to want to go on confiding in her.

It is the same with our children. An understanding parent recognizes when a child is feeling bad, and tells him so. Mother or father doesn't brush aside the feelings, or scold the child for having them, but gives him the sympathy and comfort he needs. In general, when parents acknowledge their child's feelings in this way, they make it safe for the child to express himself honestly and openly, and go a long way toward keeping the channels of communication open.

In our encounters with others, we seek warmth, understanding, acceptance. They, in turn, seek the same from us. The messages that we receive from other people affect our well-being, and our messages affect theirs. That's what good communication is all about: making us feel closer to another person, and drawing that person closer to us.

Looked at this way, "making ourselves understood" takes on a new significance. For only part of our meaning is ever carried by the words we say. As soon as your husband steps in the door at night, for example, you can usually tell right away what kind of day he has had—and even, perhaps, what kind of evening you can expect. The way he says "hi!", the way he takes off his coat, something about the set

Above: a toddler understands a lot of what goes on by gestures and facial expressions, if not by words. A little one can be upset by an angry confrontation between Mama and Papa.

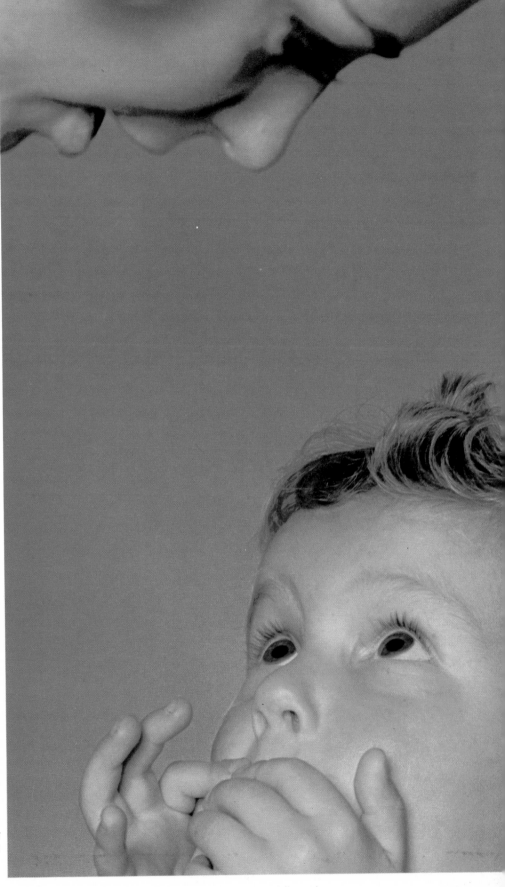

Right: you may be surprised at the fear in your child's eye at what you feel is a light scolding. Remember how big and towering you are to him, and you'll know better how he feels.

19

of his body, or the look on his face tells you plainly how he is feeling. That's the way it is with all of us. We talk with our voices, it's true, but we converse with our whole body.

So important is this "body language" that psychologist Albert Mehrabian maintains it accounts for over 90 per cent of our communication with others. It follows, then, that the more sensitive we are to such nonverbal signals, the better we will be at responding to others.

Sometimes this is easy. If your husband arrives home with the news that he has just had a raise, his jaunty air and broad grin back his words to the hilt, and the message comes through loud and clear, "I'm feeling great. My boss proved he values me."

Unfortunately, our messages are not always so clear. All too often, words say something different from body language. "How was your day?" your husband asks. "Fine," you reply; but the tenseness of your muscles as you bustle about the kitchen says entirely the opposite. Now your husband may wonder how to react: to the words, or to the nonverbal message? If he takes your "fine" literally—or if he dodges the issue entirely by retiring behind his newspaper—you are going to feel misunderstood. "Can't he see I'm tired out?" you may

You have a nagging headache, and your daughter insists on playing her newly learned tune for you—so you fly off the handle and rail at her. It's natural for you to show temper sometimes, and it can easily be put right if you later explain or apologize sincerely. In fact, making up can draw you both closer to one another.

think. Then, because you feel misunderstood, you may not feel much like understanding him either. Communication grinds to a halt, or deteriorates into conflict.

Why do we sometimes say one thing and mean another? There may be many reasons. Most of us fall into the habit of saying what we think we ought to say, or what we think others want to hear, so that they will think well of us. We may be afraid of being unacceptable or unlovable if we reveal our true feelings. We may hesitate to be honest, for fear of the other person's reactions. Perhaps we simply want to avoid hurting anyone's feelings. Sometimes it seems easier to cover up than to try to analyze emotions that could prove hard to handle. Maybe we just expect the person who loves us to know automatically how we feel, without our having to put it into words. The trouble is that, no matter how hard we try to mask them, our true feelings will still come through on the nonverbal wavelength.

Children are especially sensitive to this nonverbal language. When mother's words say one thing, and her body language another, a child senses that something is amiss. He can't quite put his finger on it, though, and he becomes confused.

That doesn't mean that you have to be

totally open with your children—or anyone
else—all the time. But, even if you want to
keep certain feelings to yourself, maybe
because they would be hurtful, you can still
be honest about having them. "I've had a
terrible day, and I really don't feel like
talking to anyone right now," might be
difficult to say, but it's more honest than
muttering, "Nothing. Just go away."

In general, we are very bad at expressing
our true feelings to our children. We don't
like to admit that we feel angry, tired, dis-
couraged, or whatever, for fear of seeming
somehow weak and less-than-perfect in their
eyes. We are afraid of losing their respect if
we admit our mistakes. But children need
contact with real people, not with saints.
If we hide our feelings, and cover up our
mistakes, our children will know it, and may
ultimately lose faith in us. If, on the other
hand, we have the courage to admit to our
human weaknesses, they are likely to respect
our honesty, and trust us more, not less.

It's natural for parents to make mistakes
in child-rearing, just as they make mistakes
in other areas of their lives. The burden of
having to feel and do the right thing all the
time can be a tremendous strain. Far better,
then, to accept that sometimes we are bound
to overreact, to fly off the handle at the least
provocation, to accuse a child wrongly of
some misbehavior, to threaten and deliver
punishments that weren't deserved. We need
to recognize that it is perfectly all right to
apologize to our child when we know we
have reacted too severely. This in no way
diminishes our authority. Rather, it helps
the child see us as the normal, fallible
human beings we are. When parents cannot
bring themselves to admit that they have
been mistaken, it is disturbing to the child.
He feels the injustice of their treatment, but
is not equipped to understand it.

Just as children are sensitive to the feelings
that lie behind our words, they are also
quick to note discrepancies between what
we say and what we do—and it is what we
do that carries the greatest weight. If mother
tries to teach Johnny not to hit her by

Will your child be out-
going and quick to make
friends? Will she be a
little pensive and slow-
moving, or he always so
ready for adventure?
The unique individual
that your child is shows
up early—and you'll all
be happier if you accept
and appreciate his or
her personality as it is.

Left: it's important to baby that father takes an active interest in him, and a role in caring for him. What a wonderful sense of security when Daddy holds him close, even if he has to share attention with a phone conversation.

Right: Is it pain? Fear? Just plain frustration? It's hard to tell at first, but soon the way a baby cries will help tell you what's wrong. Don't forget that crying is the infant's only means of communication.

hitting him right back, the lesson is doomed to failure. Similarly, all the lectures and admonitions in the world on the need for honesty won't influence a child's thinking half as much as hearing his father regale Uncle George with the story of how he fudged his tax return. We should not forget how important an example our actions and behavior are to a child—and that's a channel of communication open 24 hours a day.

Good communication, then, means making an effort to be honest with ourselves, and then sending out the kind of message that reflects our honest feeling. It means picking up another person's message, and the meaning behind that message. It means sending back the reply that shows we have understood. It means listening—not half-listening. It means looking directly at the

other person. We need only try conversing with our back to someone to realize how important eye contact is. Finally, it means focusing on the other person as he is, not as we think he should be.

This last point is important. One of the hardest things in the world for a parent to do is to see his child as the unique individual that he is. Instead, we tend to see our children in the light of our own experiences, needs, and values. Lively parents might find it hard to accept a quiet, slow-moving youngster. A father who wanted an athlete for a son may be disappointed when his child turns out to be bookish. A mother who has always regretted a lack of confidence in herself may be hard on her shy daughter.

The tragedy is that parents who hang onto their own disappointments may never

learn to appreciate what a wonderful child they have. Their concern with what their child lacks can blind them to the unique qualities that he does possess. If communicated to the child, as it is bound to be, their disappointment can do untold damage to his self-esteem. All children need acceptance if they are to function at their best, and each child longs, above all, for the approval of the two most important beings in his life.

The greatest gift we can give our children is acceptance of them as they are—letting them know that the way they are is just fine with us. A child whose self-esteem is high will have the confidence to be his own person, to resist the kind of outside pressures that parents fear may influence or harm him, and to concentrate on realizing his full potential. If you can look at your child and accept him

for what he is—not what you think he could or should be—you will appreciate his special talents and abilities, and you will find great satisfaction in his uniqueness.

Accepting a child as he is doesn't mean we should accept everything he does, but it does mean drawing a clear distinction between a child's behavior, and the child himself. When a child misbehaves, we all too often respond by making judgments of him rather than of what he has done. "You naughty boy!" we exclaim when Jimmy pinches his little sister. "How can you be so clumsy!" we cry when he knocks his glass of milk off the table. "No, stupid, I just told you not to do it like that," says Dad, helping Louis with his homework. All these reactions, if repeated often enough, can eat away at a child's self-respect. On the other

25

hand, if he can feel loved and valued for himself, in spite of the fact that his behavior sometimes makes us angry, he will feel secure enough to develop toward maturity in his own way. We help most if we try to understand his temperament, and give him the kind of support and guidance he needs.

The most important function of communication, then, is communicating our love—and it begins from the moment a child is born. Long before a baby understands words, he gathers countless impressions about himself and the world around him from the way he is treated. When his mother picks him up tenderly, holds him close, cuddles him, and speaks to him in soft, loving tones, she communicates many things—in part that he is lovable, and the world is a friendly, welcoming place. If a baby finds that he will be fed when he is hungry, changed when he is soiled and uncomfortable, and held when he is frightened, he learns to trust those who care for him. Out of these early experiences, he gains a basic faith in existence that is vital to his healthy emotional development.

How can parents help their baby develop this basic sense of trust and security? First, they have to know what kind of needs the baby has, and what kind of behavior he can respond to. The newborn infant is dependent on his parents for the satisfaction of almost all his needs. When he gets hungry, cold, wet, tired, frustrated, or sick, he has needs that must be met. However, he can't tell anyone about his condition, so his parents have to make a special effort in learning how to decode his nonverbal messages.

In the beginning of his life, crying is the only means a baby has of letting his parents know something is wrong. If babies did not have this means of communication, many would die from undetected ailments. Crying is baby's signal that he needs something—it is a cry for help. By looking and listening to your baby, you will gradually develop a sensitivity to his needs. For instance, you will notice that he has different ways of crying, and these differences will give you a clearer idea of what he is expressing. Is he screaming from hunger, or wailing miserably because he has swallowed too much wind? Is he in

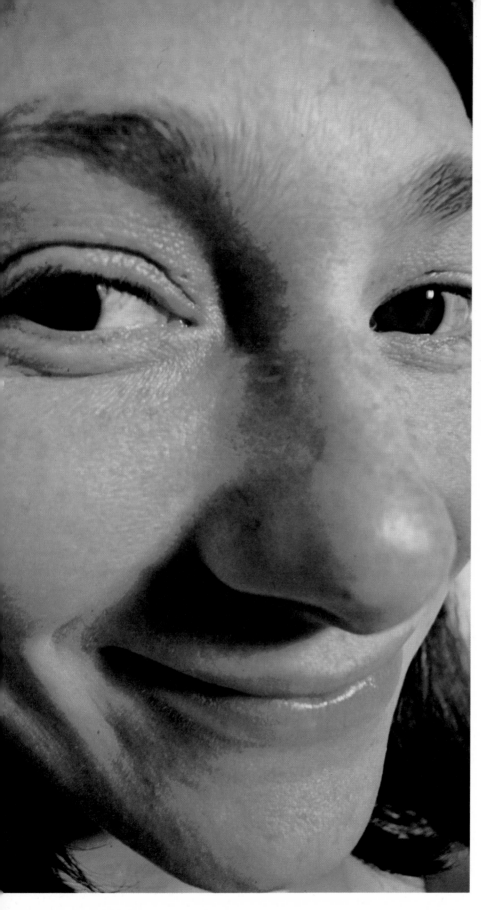

Pretty as she is (above)
her baby will see her
in a rather scary dis-
tortion (left)—but her
baby will still love
and respond to her more
than to anyone else.

pain, or simply wet and uncomfortable? Is he lonely or bored, and just in need of a good cuddle? To a new mother, these questions may seem unanswerable. But before long, she will probably have forgotten that she ever had such worries. For the more closely attentive she is to her baby, and the more she gets to know him, the easier she finds it to interpret his needs.

Physical contact is a primary way of communicating a feeling of well-being to your baby. Studies have shown that babies who were placed in crowded institutions, where they did not get adequate handling and fondling, did not develop properly. In some cases, the infants became sickly, and even died. Mother love, expressed in touching, cuddling, and speaking, is as essential to a baby as food and drink.

This physical contact needs to be accompanied by a clear expression of a mother's positive feelings toward her baby. A baby has an extraordinary ability to sense how his mother views her contact with him. When she strokes his head and holds his hand, plays with his feet and legs, shows delight in his soft, smooth skin and dimpled toes, responds to his gurgles of delight, and focuses on him alone and fully, the baby feels her warmth, and senses how much he is valued. This warm responsiveness comes across not only when a mother is feeding, changing, or bathing her baby, but also at many other times—when she gives him a friendly grin, a cheery word, or tickle as she passes his crib, chats with him, hugs and kisses him, sings to him, and plays with him. Through all these warm contacts, the baby comes to feel that he can count on his mother's response to him. He also needs to develop the same kind of trust in others, especially his father. Whether father helps with feeding, bathing, or changing diapers, or simply plays with his baby, he can increase that vital sense of confidence without which the baby will find it hard to take his first steps toward independence.

Some fathers don't feel comfortable with very young babies, and only come into

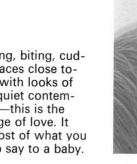

Laughing, biting, cuddling, faces close together with looks of joy or quiet contemplation—this is the language of love. It says most of what you need to say to a baby.

28

their own when their children are older. It is important not to discourage your husband from becoming involved simply because he holds the baby a bit awkwardly, or looks perilously close to letting her slip in the bath. Fathers at first often feel anxious about holding the baby, and criticism from you on how he handles her will only make matters worse. If your husband is a little hamfisted, don't worry. He will improve with practice. He may even become something of an expert. Most importantly, the baby will thrive on his attention.

The baby's sensitivity to his parents' feelings and actions works the other way, too. When mother is tired, irritated, or anxious, baby is fussy, fretful, and uncooperative. Then, the more he fusses or yells, the more tense his poor mother becomes.

"My first few weeks at home with my baby were a nightmare," reports one mother. "Julia never seemed to stop crying, and the more she cried, the more hopeless I became. I felt totally incompetent, and convinced that I wasn't cut out for motherhood at all. I began to wish I'd never had a baby. Julia seemed to know what I was thinking, and became even harder to handle. That made me feel guilty as well, and even more miserable."

Many women will recognize and sympathize with this woman's feelings. A new mother has to cope with so many warring emotions that it is not surprising if she feels panicky, inadequate, and downright resentful at times. No matter how adorable her baby is, she is likely to feel uneasy at the thought of his utter dependence on her, and at the prospect of caring for his needs for a long time to come. She may feel that she will never again be alone with her husband, and never again have time for herself, or be able to go out when she feels like it. Then, too, there is the heavy pressure of feeling that the way she handles her baby now will have far-reaching effects on his emotional health in later years.

Some mothers genuinely find infants less

interesting than children. They may feel ill-at-ease in the intimate physical contact of the early months, and only begin to enjoy their children when they become a little more independent. Babies, too, differ in their reactions. Right from the start, some babies are placid, quiet, and easy to handle, while others are highly active, tense, or sensitive. Some babies adapt easily to changes in environment and food, for example, while others squawk and bellow at every new experience. All too often, a mother blames her own incompetence for reactions that may simply be a result of her baby's special temperament. Getting to know the particular characteristics of her baby's personality can be one of the most rewarding aspects of motherhood, once a mother is relaxed enough to appreciate them.

No matter what his temperament, however, every baby is bound to be demanding and difficult at times, and it's undoubtedly wearing to spend hours of every day—and especially every night—feeding and changing and walking a fretful baby. "I would never have thought it possible," says one mother, "but now, when I read about parents hitting their babies, I can actually understand how it could happen. One day when my baby had been particularly cranky and difficult, I felt so downright helpless and angry that I actually shook her hard, and almost threw her down in her crib. Then I burst into tears myself, and couldn't stop howling until my husband came and managed to calm both of us down." Such are the moments when husbands can come to the rescue most helpfully. The relationship between mother and baby is an intense one, from which both sometimes need an escape. If father can step in with a more relaxed attitude when there has been a particularly painful buildup of emotion, it can help enormously. What about when the baby is driving you to distraction, and father isn't around? Once you're sure there is nothing wrong, it may be best to put the baby in his crib, and let him cry for the time it takes to call a friend, and relieve some of your feelings by getting them

expressed. You'll then be able to manage.

The important thing to remember is that such angry feelings are just as much part of parenthood as the spontaneous welling up of warmth and love for that tiny being snuggled close against you, the joy at seeing his first smile, or the fun of watching his early attempts to crawl. Occasional angry outbursts, or moments of fatigue, irritation, or tension in dealing with your baby are not going to cause him permanent damage. As long as the general tenor of your relationship with your baby is reasonably loving and attentive, he will thrive. When the times of warmth and love outnumber the times of disinterest or irritation, when a hug or a kiss follows an impatient scolding, the baby gets the message.

A real problem may arise, however, if parents begin to attribute all kinds of unrealistic motives to their baby's behavior. "He won't give me a moment's peace," we may wail when the baby wakes us up for the umpteenth time, or "he's out to drive me crazy." This is unfair. The baby is not yet capable of such motivation. His reasons for crying are much more basic. He cries because he is hungry, or colicky, or because a diaper pin is sticking into him. When we begin to distort the meaning of the baby's behavior, our ability to be a responsive, communicative parent is diminished. The baby is sending out adequate messages, but we are not receiving them accurately. Instead of listening, we are distorting, and the message gets lost in the midst of our resentment.

While acknowledging our feelings of anger or worry over the baby's crying, we should not be tempted into believing that the baby is deliberately setting out to make us feel that way—a motivation that he could not possibly have. Only by trying to understand what a baby's behavior actually means *to him* can we start to achieve good communication. By developing this sensitivity first of all to our baby's needs, we will lay the foundations for a happy and open relationship that can continue and grow through childhood and into adolescence.

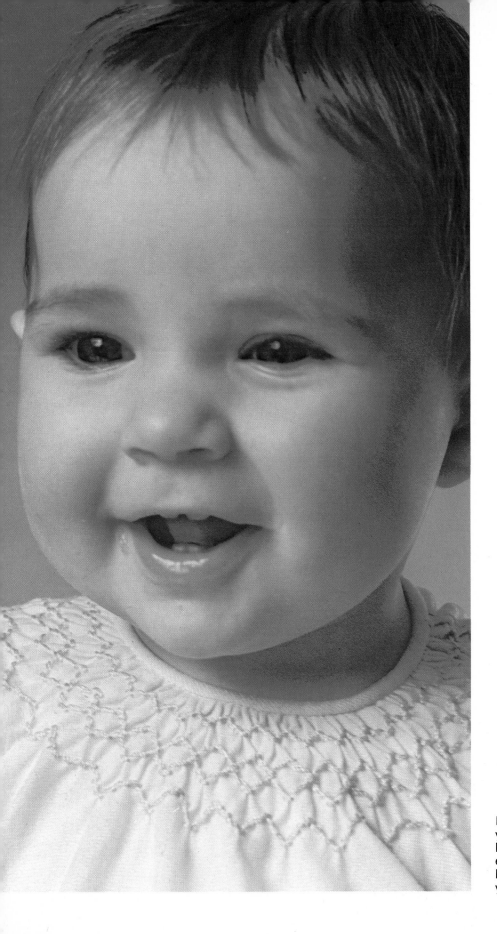

Does anything renew
your faith and hope in
life as much as the
endearing, appealing,
heart-warming smile of
your beloved baby?

31

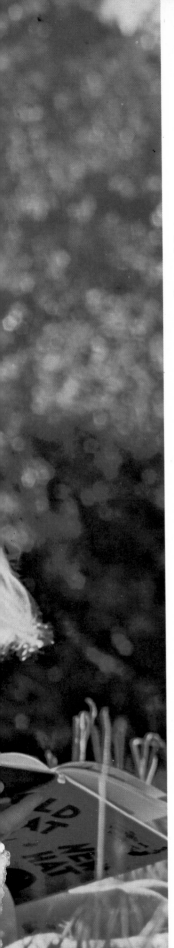

Learning to Talk

2

"I see kitty cat", she cries in delight—and you are delighted, too. For you know that she's not only enjoying the story and the pictures in the book you're reading, but is also improving her language skill. Reading with your child is a shared experience that pays off in big dividends for her.

"Mick!" cried Brian, clutching the bars of his playpen. His parents looked puzzled. "Mick! Mick! Mick!" shouted Brian more insistently. He could tell that his parents were not getting the message. They knew that he used this word, one of half-a-dozen in his vocabulary, to mean milk, his favorite toy giraffe, and his older brother Michael. So his mother said, picking up the giraffe, "Do you want Mick?" Brian's exasperation grew. "Mick! Mick!" he shrieked. "Here's some nice milk," tried Dad, lifting Brian up and offering him his bottle. Wrong again. "Do you want to play with Michael?" asked his mother. Right at last. Michael, who had been playing noisily in the next room, came running in, and Brian beamed.

Although a baby may be able to use only a few words at first, his understanding is well in advance of his speech. He knows what he is trying to say even if he cannot say the words for it, and it is up to us to do our best to understand what he wants to put across. In this way, we encourage him to make the switchover from wholly nonverbal communication to using words to communicate effectively. If, on the other hand, we fail to respond, give up after the first or second attempt to understand, or assume we know what the baby wants despite his continuing protests, he may get to feel that talking isn't such a worthwhile accomplishment after all.

Gurgling, chuckling, and cooing are among a baby's earliest attempts to express his feelings. At first, he delights in making his own happy, natural sounds, and this is an important part of his development; but the process of playing with his own sounds is not enough without a response from others.

33

Studies have shown that a baby will make far more sounds when his parents smile or talk to him than when they just stand silently by his crib. Physical contact, loving attention, and plenty of warm encouragement are what make a baby want to talk, and when his parents and other members of the family chat to him and delight in his responses, they provide the feedback he needs to convert his sounds into actual words.

One of the strongest urges a baby has is the urge to imitate. By the time he is about a year old, he will not merely be listening and playing with sounds, but will have begun to imitate the particular sounds his mother makes. Like Brian, he may have heard his mother say "milk", and he says "mick" as the nearest he can come to it. Gradually he begins to associate certain sounds and objects, and learns to ask for things he wants in words rather than by gestures. At first, of course, both parent and child still need to rely heavily on explanatory actions, gestures, facial expressions and tones of voice, to back up the words. Before long, though, the child begins to produce simple statements and questions that are not just repetition, but his own invention. To his own and his parents' delight, he has begun to communicate with others on a new and higher level.

The development of language is one of the most mysterious and wonderful skills that a child acquires in his early years. As the main tool that will help him develop his intelligence, it is crucial to his future intellectual growth. So how can a mother help her child to absorb, learn, and enjoy using words?

The most important way of all, as we have already seen, is to respond to your baby's early attempts to talk, and, of course, to chat to him whenever you are together. As you walk your baby along in his stroller, take him shopping, or to visit friends, you can point out familiar objects along the way, talking to him in simple words and short sentences about what you are doing, and where you are going. As you bathe and dress him, you can name the various parts of his body, and the clothes he is going to wear.

Soon you will find that your child's favorite question is "What's that?", and you will be busy naming new objects for him all day long. You may have to say the same word for him several times over, but by patiently repeating—and by getting him to show you what he wants when you don't understand his words—you will give him the gentle encouragement he needs to go on trying to express himself through language.

Once your toddler knows certain words you can ask him to bring you, say, his cup, or his socks, or a packet of crackers in the supermarket. At bedtime you can talk over with him some of the things you did during the day, or he could help you turn the pages of a brightly colored picture book and talk about familiar objects.

Little children love all kinds of rhymes and verses and songs. Rhythm has been bred into them from their earliest weeks in the womb, when they were first lulled by the regular, soothing beat of their mother's heart. Rhythm can help you manage a boisterous toddler—for example, try singing an order rather than saying it. Even young babies will delight in nursery rhymes like, "This little piggy" and "pat-a-cake." It is often by learning to recognize the familiar sounds of such jingles, and playing his part in the game, that a baby begins to understand language. He may start using a word from a game to tell you he wants to play that game. Most toddlers, too, delight in nonsense words like the ones they use as they chatter away to themselves.

A two-year-old's made-up words ("a strokey cat" or "a smutter of cream") can be so delightful that they find a permanent place in the family's vocabulary. But what about baby talk? Should parents go along with this, or insist right from the start that a baby say "dog" instead of "bow-wow," or "cow" instead of "moo-moo?" Most experts agree that it is better to use the correct word so as to make life easier for the child when he goes to school, and starts learning to read. But there is probably no harm in using baby talk sometimes, until your child is able

"Here's my nose. Now, where is yours?" Showing baby the parts of the body can be a little question-and-answer game—and before long, baby will know where to point and what to call things by name. It's one of the best ways to teach baby how to talk.

Birth to 18 Months

Approximate Age	Activity	Vocal Reactions	Social Reactions
Birth	Stares at lights, colored mobiles, colored pictures and nearby face	Crying is usual language	Loves to be picked up and cuddled
4 weeks	Starts to follow people and large objects with eyes Grips objects on contact Enjoys bath	Little throaty noises from time to time	Usually calms down when spoken to, especially by deep masculine voice Usually will get still and listen to new sounds
8 weeks	When placed on abdomen, intermittently lifts chin and head; when held in sitting position, may lift head upright	Vocalizes with growing variety of sounds, especially when talked to	Smiles at people and some sounds Enjoys being held and spoken or sung to
4 months	Lifts head up and pushes body up on arms when placed on abdomen Grasps and holds rattles Watches his fingers	Laughs and coos Bubbles, gurgles, may cough and make other sounds to hear own voice	Recognizes parents and others close to him Enjoys being with people Enjoys being pulled up by hands; likes rhythm
6 months	May begin to sit up without support Rolls over by self Shakes and bangs rattle Places objects in mouth	Laughs, coos, and vocalizes a great deal	Continues to enjoy people; may cry when they leave the room Enjoys sitting up and looking around

When will your baby first smile at you? Learn to talk? To walk? No one can say for sure, because patterns of development vary widely from child to child. However, this chart gives an idea of an average baby's progress for the first 18 months.

to say the correct word easily and happily.

In the same way, it can be tactless to correct a child immediately when he says "poon" for "spoon," "toogah" for "sugar," or "seed" instead of "saw." Imagine yourself trying to speak a foreign language, and having your first hesitant words of French greeted by a roar of laughter, or an irate attempt to correct your pronunciation. Chances are, you wouldn't be eager to risk a second snub. A child whose parents constantly point out his mistakes in speech may become shy and frightened about talking at all. If, on the other hand, you say the word correctly when replying, or later in the conversation, he will soon begin saying it the right way.

Even if he is not yet able to talk, by the time a child is $1\frac{1}{2}$ or 2 he can understand simple messages about how his parents feel, and whether or not they approve of what he is doing. He knows what it means when mother says, "No, Mommy doesn't like that," or "No, Joanne, that's Daddy's," "That's

Approximate Age	Activity	Vocal Reactions	Social Reactions
9 *months*	Pulls self up in playpen Begins to creep Sits up well May hold own bottle Often walks if held by both hands	Makes many sounds and enjoys hearing own voice May say "Mama" and "Dada"	Loves to play peekaboo Enjoys being wheeled in carriage; sits up and looks at everything If taught, will wave "bye-bye"
12 *months*	May stand alone for a moment without support Walks held by one hand Enjoys throwing things down from high chair or out of playpen	Usually says a few simple words such as "light," "Mama," "Dada," and "bow-wow"	May be shy of strangers Responds to "No! No!" Much interested in other children, dogs, autos, etc. Loves carriage-walks
15 *months*	Walks independently, but usually unsteadily Creeps up stairs and pulls self up on low chairs Enjoys picture books and colorful magazines Usually watches TV Loves playing with boxes and pots and pans	Talks a great deal, but often not understandable Imitates sounds and occasionally rhythm	Often points or indicates by voice what he desires May indicate by sounds when he is urinating or having a bowel movement
18 *months*	Walks well with fairly good coordination Climbs easily up stairs; walks down holding on Throws or rolls ball Pulls and pushes toys; plays with toy dolls and animals Carries out simple directions	Usually has about 15 words in vocabulary Often names objects he sees, including those in picture books	Usually very social

hot," or "That will hurt, Joanne." But what happens before that? How can you communicate effectively to your crawler or toddler that it is dangerous to tug at the lamp cord, or play near the elevator, that he musn't touch Daddy's watch, or grab Mommy's best china?

First of all, we need to recognize the young child's tremendous need for freedom to explore. He has to find out about things, to touch them, smell them, taste them, and test them out. This is the way he learns about his world. For him, that world is brimful of new things that he is only just beginning to discover. Those discoveries can be either exciting or threatening, depending on how his parents react to his investigations. Too many "no's" and "don't's" may not only frustrate, but also discourage him in his desire to learn. If we continually snatch things away from him, or scold him when he explores, he may get the idea that it is wrong to want to learn, and that his parents love him better when he isn't being curious.

The goal, then, is to find ways of preventing a child from harmful, or destructive behavior without crushing his initiative, to provide him with activities that can be both satisfying to him, and acceptable to other members of the family. It helps if you start out by planning a part of your home (or a corner of the backyard) where your toddler can be free to explore objects that interest him without damaging anything. Take away any valuables you are anxious to protect, make sure the area is safe, and that it includes a low shelf or shallow box of toys and other items that can be safely investigated. That way your child will learn that there are places at home where he is allowed to play freely. If your toddler starts playing with something forbidden, try offering him a safe substitute—some empty cartons instead of your cosmetics, an old magazine instead of your precious books, a big sheet of wrapping paper to draw on instead of the wallpaper.

Remember, the less often you say "no", the more likely your toddler is to heed you when you do say it. So the next step is to limit your "no's" to times when they are absolutely essential. Try making a mental list of the objects that you can't allow your child to touch, and the rules that you consider must always be followed, keeping the list as short as possible. For every parent the list will vary, of course, but the items with highest priority are bound to be those that concern your child's health or safety—poking at electric sockets, or reaching up to touch the hot stove, for example.

In such cases you have to say "no", and your child must know you mean it. Your stern expression and disapproving tone will help, but at this age, you need to back them up by action. As you firmly say "no!" pick your child up and carry him away from the socket, or grasp his hand and lead him out of the kitchen. Then he will know that you are in earnest. Nevertheless, he may still wander back to the socket—maybe poking the other hand at it this time--to see if your reaction will still be the same. Of course, it should be. It may be scant consolation as

There are times when a child's natural curiosity and seemingly total lack of fear—often based on lack of knowledge—puts him or her in a dangerous situation. You'll just have to accept the fact that you'll have some scares over your child's safety, and learn how to handle the emergencies.

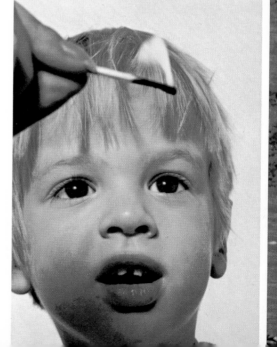

you race after your toddler for the umpteenth time, but he really isn't bent on deliberately defying you. "Believe it or not," says pediatrician Dr. Lee Salk, "your child is behaving like a well-disciplined scientist who is testing a series of hypotheses to find out exactly what is causing your reaction." Maybe your budding Einstein will need to poke at all the light plugs in the room before he is satisfied, but provided your reaction is the same every time, he will end up learning a valuable lesson in safety, as well as respecting your ability to set limits on his behavior.

Consistency is vital. If we are inconsistent, sometimes saying "no" and sometimes "yes" to certain behavior; saying "no" half-a-dozen times, only to give in wearily on the seventh; or letting our "stop that!" reach fever pitch before stepping in to enforce it, the child becomes anxious and confused. He doesn't know where he is. We are unpredictable. He can't work out what our limits really are. Children look to us for guidance. They want to try things out, but they need plainly established limits. If the limits shift too often, or are never set up at all, a child may feel that his parents don't care what he does or what happens to him. He may then misbehave twice as much simply to find out how far he can go before we start caring.

It will help your toddler to respect your "no" or "don't touch" if you hold him firmly while you say it and turn his head toward you. Just as adults need to look at each other when they talk, communication with young children is always more effective if you get down to child level, face to face. Then your child recognizes that what you have to say is important, and he is much more likely to pay attention.

Does this mean that punishment is never justified? How about spanking, for example? Spanking certainly pounds a message home, but what message? Unfortunately, it tells the child more about your behavior than about his. Remember what a powerful example your actions are. Parents who hit their child or rage at him for his mistakes

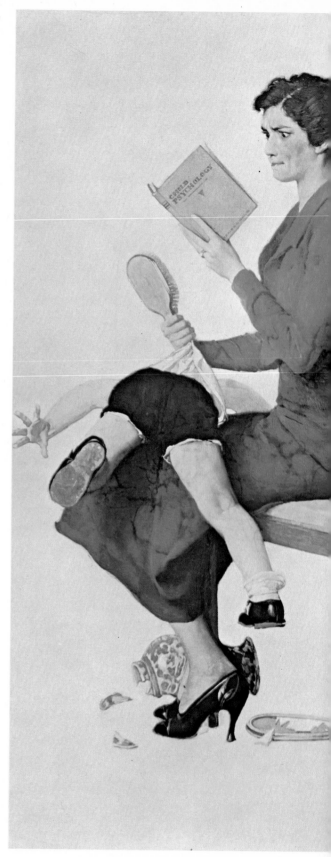

To spank or not to spank—that is one of the toughest decisions for parents. This painting by Norman Rockwell takes the humorous view, but it's a serious matter. One thing to keep in mind is that generally, spanking does not teach discipline, and can breed untoward fear.

get pretty upset when the same child keeps picking on his little sister, or punches other children in school. But the child is only doing what he has been taught by your example that as good as said: "If you don't like what someone does, hit him."

Spanking doesn't teach discipline. It teaches fear, deviousness, and aggression. Put yourself in the child's place. How would you like to be slapped by a person who is bigger and more powerful than yourself, someone you can't slap back? How would you like being slapped for doing something you did not know was wrong? Because it can be extremely frightening for a child to be spanked, spanking is only appropriate in the most extreme circumstances. If your child darts out into the street, for example, a swift slap will convey strongly that this is not to be done. But let's face it. However much we try to rationalize that the slap was "for the child's own good", it was really administered out of fear—our own fear for the child's safety.

Sometimes we try to justify ourselves when we slap from fright or from sheer exasperation by saying: "That'll teach you not to be so naughty!", or "Mommy had to do that to make you understand". We would do better to be honest, and, while giving the child a hug of apology, say, "I'm sorry. I shouldn't have hit you, but I was angry. People sometimes do silly things when they're angry." This won't give the child permission to run across the street or misbehave again, but it will teach him that people are human, and may do things for which they're sorry.

Most of us start out with the best of intentions regarding spanking, only to falter in the fact of practical parenthood. "I was determined never to hit my children," says many a mother, "until one day . . . ." Even so, an occasional slap is not going to destroy a child's well-being. Provided we apologize sincerely when we overreact, we leave the way open for better ways of communicating. Fortunately, children don't dwell on single incidents. They know when we are frightened or at the end of our patience, and they are

The two-to-three-year-old starts asserting his independence, and it will smooth things if you offer him some choices in which he can show his individuality. One way is to let him choose which color shirt he wants to wear that day; but don't confuse the issue with too many alternatives. He may then react by falling back on a stubborn "no" again.

perfectly ready to forgive, forget, and make up.

Of course, parents don't want to be feared by their children as dispensers of harsh punishments. We want to enjoy parenthood, and reap the benefits of rearing a loving child. It is a challenge to find ways of helping a child learn the necessary rules and regulations without becoming a tyrant. Being respected without being feared is far more rewarding for a parent.

We can make the job much more fun if we devote more time and energy to telling a child what he can do, rather than what he can't. If Johnny wants to play with his ball in the living room, you could say, "You can play in the backyard," rather than listing all the places where he musn't throw the ball. So much of a toddler's anger and frustration comes from discovering all the things he can't master because he is too little or too inexperienced. He needs your help in providing tasks at which he can succeed; clothes he can put on by himself; a stool or box he can stand on to reach faucets and closet hooks; dishes and glasses that won't break; sturdy furniture and toys; and space for running and climbing.

It is important to remember, too, that praise and encouragement are always far more effective than nagging and scolding. Children are bound to make mistakes, and to forget some of our rules, especially at first.

But they want to learn, they want to act like grownups, they want to win the approval of those they love. A big smile and a hug when Mary helps Daddy put her toys away, an occasional "That's fine!" or "What lovely clean hands!" are irresistible encouragements. When you love your child and he knows it, when you show your pleasure and approval of certain ways of behaving, he will want to keep on trying to please you.

Of course, even a child who feels approved of and is eager to please can have his uncooperative moments. Sometime between the ages of $1\frac{1}{2}$ and 3—usually around $2\frac{1}{2}$—your toddler is likely to hit the notorious phase known as "the terrible twos". Suddenly, he's the one who's saying all the "no's". Open rebellion is the order of the day, and mother is his chief adversary in the battle for independence.

How can a mother handle the two-year-old who refuses to do anything she asks, who

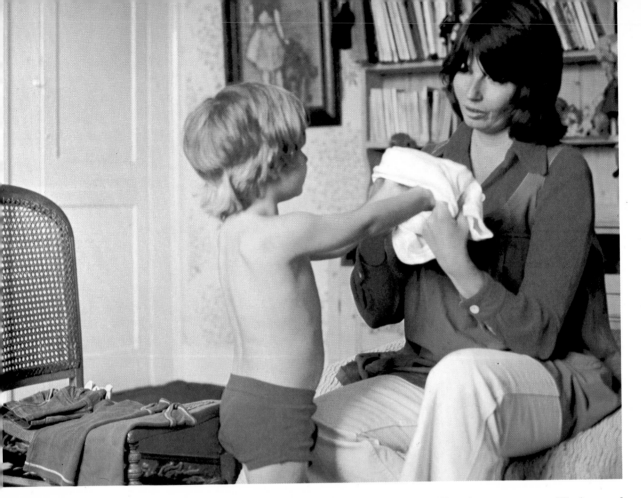

embarrasses her in public by kicking and screaming when she won't buy him a candy bar, who insists on doing everything himself one minute, and demands that she do it the next? Well, just as with your baby, it helps to understand what this behavior means to your child. The two-year-old is busily engaged in developing a sense of his own identity, a feeling of himself as an individual separate from his mother. His defiance and rebellion are important ways of practicing that separateness, and developing his sense of self. Up until now, he has constantly been running up against the barrier of his parents' "no"—a "no" they can enforce by thwarting his activity. When he experiments with "no's" of his own, he is beginning to feel himself as having some of the power that previously belonged solely to his parents.

Unless we are aware of this new-found need for independence, a two-year-old's behavior can sometimes be baffling. Gary's mother was about to sprinkle some sugar on his cornflakes. "Don't want sugar!" shouted Gary; but he howled with rage when his mother took the sugar bowl away. A 2 or 2½-year-old will often say "no" or "I won't!" to something, and then go right ahead and do it. It is as if his need to practice his independence must come first, but he doesn't want to have to lose out on something he enjoys because of it.

Exasperating and difficult though his contrariness may be, it is important to realize that your toddler is not deliberately "out to get you". He is just trying out a new kind of behavior, and seeing how it feels. By declaring his separateness, he is beginning to feel his own strength, and to become less dependent, which is what growing up is all about. If we are unwilling to allow him to experiment with new behavior, he may become submissive or overdependent, or find spiteful ways to disobey. In either case, he will not be working toward his full potential. Of course, the question of how

43

much or how little leeway to give a child is an individual one that must be worked out between each parent and child. But when we begin to feel threatened, undermined, or infuriated by a two-year-old's behavior, it can help to remind ourselves of the purpose of his defiance. Parents who see their rebellious toddler as the enemy, and treat him accordingly, set up what could be a lifelong battle that will damage all of you.

What, then, are the practical ways of allowing a two-year-old to experiment with his developing sense of self, while still preserving your sanity? Some mothers have found that, since their toddler will invariably do the opposite of what he is asked, it helps to make an opposite request: "Don't put those shoes on," they say, works better than, "Come along, Barbara, we'll just get your shoes on and you can go out to play." Mothers who feel that this technique is too false might prefer to make up a few games that allow a toddler to practice perfectly legitimate "no's": "Is your ice-cream blue?" you could ask, or "Does the cow say 'quack-quack'?"

A more positive approach would be to let your child practice his independence by giving him choices—so long as you intend to stick by his decision. Rather than just giving him his breakfast, you could offer him two different cereals and say, "Which is your favorite today?" or "Do you want milk or juice this morning?" Keep the choices as clear as you can. "Which shirt do you like best today—the red one or the green one?", is better than saying, "What do you want to wear today?", which could produce a stubborn "nothing!"

Adding a few words of explanation to your requests also helps: "Shall we stop playing now so we have time for a story before bed?" However, explanations must be brief. For example, "we must stop playing now because it's nearly bedtime, and if we don't get you bathed and ready for bed before Daddy gets home, I won't have time to cook his dinner, and he won't be able to read you a story",

What to do when your toddler has a tantrum in the middle of the supermarket? The best course is to pick him up and talk to him soothingly while taking him outside. Alone, you can probably find out why he was so upset, and get him calmed down. This will increase his trust in your ability to help him.

is bewildering. It can leave a child wondering what you really are getting at. Better, too, to avoid the kind of request that leaves you open to challenge. "Drink your milk, or we won't go to the park this afternoon," tempts your toddler to see if you will carry out your threat, and may leave you wondering how you can. Similarly, a wistful, "You will be good when Auntie Marjorie comes today, won't you, honey?", suggests that he can say "no"—which he probably will.

All too often we make near impossible demands—"be quiet!", "sit still!"—without explaining why, or offering an alternative. Other times, we deliberately allow ourselves to be drawn into battle. "You must be hungry—you haven't eaten a thing all day!" we cry, or "No, Andy, you don't want an ice cream just before lunch." It can be hard to start thinking of our toddler as an individual with feelings of his own, but we could try by saying, "I'm feeling hungry and I'm going to eat some cheese. Would you like to share it?" Or, "I know you want an ice cream, but I can't let you have one right before lunch. Let's see how fast we can race home and set the table."

Positive suggestions are always wiser than direct commands. "Let's get the pink soap and wash our hands together," works better than, "Go wash your hands." "If we hurry, we might see the men digging the road again," could encourage a child who refuses to put on his coat to go out. If bedtime is a battle, try "Let's see if you can be in bed by the time this record stops." Or, "Let's be ducks and waddle to bed. I'm going to go flip-flop on my big yellow feet; are you?"

At lunchtime, a child who is absorbed in play needs at least 10 minutes warning that it is nearly time to eat. If he still won't come, try joining in a game again. "Let's be cars and drive in to lunch. Brmm! Brmm! How loud can your car go?" If you just can't see yourself entering into this kind of play, you could still suggest the idea, and confine yourself to, say, pretending to start his engine, or flag him off to a start.

The main aim during this awkward phase is to dodge head-on conflicts over behavior, while at the same time recognizing the toddler's right to his feelings. Before a child is able to put his feelings into words, he has to try to express himself by the only means he knows—kicking, biting, hitting, or screaming, if necessary—and a mother needs to acknowledge the feelings behind this rather explosive body language. Supposing Robert struggles to land a punch at his baby brother, and mother slaps him and shouts, "Stop that at once!" She has stopped the act, all right, but not the feelings behind it. Instead she could say, "O.K. I can see you're angry with John, but you can't hit your brother. You can punch your doll or this cushion because you're angry." That way, she acknowledges Robert's angry feelings, but channels those feelings into a safe and healthy outlet. Robert can express his feelings, but he hasn't hurt anyone.

That's all very well, you might say, but what happens when my child throws a tantrum in the supermarket, and there aren't any healthy outlets around? A slap may solve the situation, but will send the feelings underground to reappear in later misbehavior. Giving in is a signal that dooms you to future tantrums. In fact, the child himself may be extremely frightened by the intensity of feelings that he can't control. He needs, above all, to feel that his parents *are* in control, and are not overwhelmed by his violence.

Mother can often help best by picking him up or holding him in her arms, and talking to him calmly, so that he feels secure. If you're in the supermarket, it is a good idea to carry him outside, continuing to talk quietly to him about whatever caused the outburst. He may go on kicking and screaming, but you will gradually feel him listening as you talk. As he quietens down, he may even be able to say a few simple words about what happened. When you show your child that you accept the importance of his feelings, and are able to help him work through his anger without anyone getting hurt, you

The fond hug, the few words said with heads close together—these are ways of communicating, and of building a sense of security and psychological health in your precious child.

deepen his trust in you, and open the way for understanding on the more sophisticated level of words. It's true that some children get over their tantrums more quickly if left to themselves, but they, too, will probably come back for a hug when the storm is over, to be reassured of mother's continuing love.

The two-year-old is still only a little child. Despite his strivings for independence, the very discovery of his own separateness makes him anxious about letting his mother out of sight, just in case she shouldn't come back. Life isn't easy when you're two. The two-year-old may suddenly find himself being asked to give up so many of the comfortable, secure things of babyhood: his

bedtime bottle, his diapers, thumb sucking, or the old bit of blanket he carries around everywhere. No wonder he sometimes yearns to grow backward instead of forward. When you understand the pressures he faces, it can seem less puzzling that the toddler who has been stoutly defying you all day suddenly bursts into tears, clings to you, and won't even let you go to the bathroom without him.

Demanding and irritating, unpredictable and baffling though a two- to three-year-old may be, his is still an age of special enjoyment to parents. His spontaneous delight in the world, his eagerness to learn, his laughter and gaiety, and his irresistible charm make it impossible to be cross or serious with him for long. Of all the ways of communicating with your toddler, the most important is simply to enjoy him. By sharing his play, and delighting in his unique ways of doing and learning, you can make these years a happy dialogue between you. Children don't forget the warm experiences of early childhood. The cosy feeling of snuggling up in bed as Daddy reads a story, the excitement of helping mother roll out "real" pastry, getting to scrape the last bit of jam from the jar, all these simple pleasures are woven into a child's earliest memories. They, too, help reinforce the feeling of being loved and valued that is every child's most precious psychological possession.

Those Awkward Questions!

3

"Why is the sky blue?" "What holds the airplane up?" "Where's Africa?" "How does the wind blow?" "Where does it go?" "Why can't I marry Daddy?" "Why must I say thank you to Grandma?" "Why did Grandpa die?" "When will you die?" "Where did I come from?" "Is Daddy having a baby, too?" "Why is that lady so fat?" "Why, Mommy, why?"

There you were worrying about how your child wasn't learning to talk, and now you're busy answering numerous searching questions every day. If the two-year-old's favorite word was "no", the three-to-five's typical conversation starters are "What?", "When?", "Where?", "How?", and "Why?"—fired at you when you are in the midst of making dinner, heaving a stroller and a week's shopping into the car, or about to sink into an armchair to watch television. At moments like this, the temptation to snap, "Because I say so!" or "Not now, darling!" can overwhelm the best of us.

It *is* hard work satisfying an under-five's seemingly endless curiosity, but it can also be very rewarding. Now you and your child can really talk together, and you can enjoy seeing the world through his eyes—new and exciting. Experts agree that the effort parents make to answer their child's early questions not only gives him a head start when he gets to school, but also encourages him to go on talking to his parents about his interests and concerns. A child who is often

She's amusing herself with her book at the moment, but all too soon she'll probably be bombarding you with "why", "how", "what". This phase of growing up is the one of the endless awkward questions.

told, "Don't bother me now. Go play with your toys," or "I'll tell you when you're older. Now finish your breakfast like a good boy," may well become the child of whom parents later complain, "I don't know what's going on in that child's head. He never tells me anything."

That doesn't mean that you have to produce an instant reply on everything from household plumbing to nuclear physics. If you can provide a satisfactory answer right away, so much the better. But if questions crop up at an awkward moment, or you simply don't know the answer, it does no harm to say so. There is nothing wrong in telling a child, "I'm too busy to explain right now because we must finish the shopping. But I'll tell you when we get home"—provided, of course, you keep that promise.

We shouldn't be afraid to own up when we don't know the answer to a child's question. Better to say, "I don't know—but we can find out," than to offer an off-the-cuff explanation in the hope of safeguarding our image. A child will find out sooner or later that he has been misled, and may lose the very trust in us that we wanted to protect. Admitting our ignorance, like admitting our mistakes, can encourage a child to recognize that grownups are not remote, all-perfect beings, and that they don't know everything, but often have ways of finding the answer.

How, then, can we best reply to a child's questions, and encourage a lively, inquiring mind? When the questions are factual, it is not so difficult. The local library or museum, a few reference books on the kitchen shelf, even relatives or friends can

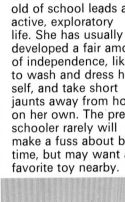

The child on the threshold of school leads an active, exploratory life. She has usually developed a fair amount of independence, liking to wash and dress herself, and take short jaunts away from home on her own. The preschooler rarely will make a fuss about bedtime, but may want a favorite toy nearby.

help us out. But there is a whole area of questioning that requires more than patience and knowledge to handle. When our child asks about God, love, sex, death, and birth, we have to come up with helpful answers. Since these are the hardest questions of all, we need to think about them in advance.

It is possible, however, to be overanxious to answer awkward questions. For instance, little Johnny comes running to mother and asks, "Mommy, where do I come from?" "Uhuh," thinks mother, "here we go," and launches into her carefully prepared account of conception, pregnancy, and birth. "Yes, Mommy," says Johnny when she's finally through, "but what I want to know is—you see, Billy says he comes from Chicago. Where do I come from?"

Libby's mother discovered another pitfall about overdoing early sex education when her daughter raced in to announce: "Mommy, Sylvie's cat just had her kittens!" Mother thought this an ideal opportunity to give her daughter all the facts of life. But Libby could hardly wait for her to finish. "Yes, and Mommy, d'you know?" she insisted excitedly, "there are three kittens and they're ever so tiny and they can't open their eyes." As far as the facts of life were concerned, Libby wasn't interested then.

The golden rule in answering an under-five's questions about sex is to answer only as much as the child asks, when he asks it. While it is important to answer spontaneously and truthfully, we need to listen carefully to the precise nature of a small child's question. Giving him too many details at once can be so bewildering that he fails to grasp the answer to his original inquiry.

A two- or three-year-old who wants to know, "Where do babies come from?" needs no more than a simple reply: "Babies come from their mommies." Maybe right away, but probably later, he will ask, "Where in their mommies?", and you can say, "In a special place just for babies, near the mother's tummy." This is better than telling a child, "You grew in mommy's tummy," which may lead to confused ideas

about babies and food being in the same place, or conception being connected with eating. Similarly, explanations about "seeds" and "planting" can be taken too literally by a child who may see this in terms of apple or watermelon seeds to be swallowed, or of someone picking up a flower seed and planting it with a trowel.

It is important to use the correct names for the organs of the body. Even when talking to a very young child you can identify the "special place in mother's body" as the *uterus*, and use the words *vagina* and *penis* in describing the sex organs. For a child who is busy picking up lots of new words, these are no harder to learn than any of the traditional substitutes. Not only are they the right words, but also they are largely free of any naughty connotations. Using them can help you talk more objectively to your child, and save him confusion later.

"How did I get there?" will probably be the next question. Again, you might at first reply simply, "Daddy put you there." But since a child may imagine that Daddy placed him, fully grown, inside his mother, it might be less confusing at this stage merely

Today there are many good educational aids for all age levels to help parents explain sex. The little girl above examines a cut-out of an animal giving birth.

Right: two preteeners—twins themselves—study a model of foetal twins.

to explain that mother has little egg cells inside her body and that, from time to time, one of these cells grows into a baby. Most children will then ask, "How does the baby get out?" "When the baby is old enough," you could say, "it comes out through a special opening between mother's legs called the vagina." This is a good time to show the child a drawing of the human body and explain where the vagina is, taking care to distinguish this "special opening" from the neighboring openings. It is also wise to explain that this opening is able to stretch wide enough to let the baby out, so that the child will not worry about birth being too painful, or hurting mother. Little girls need

52

to be reassured that they do not have babies growing in them now, that "you have to be at least as grownup as a high school girl before the cells can grow into babies." Little boys should understand that a girl carries the baby in her uterus, but that babies also need fathers to love and care for them.

Questions about father's role usually come last of all. At first, you can simply explain that a cell from the father's body joins the cell in the mother's body, and starts the baby growing. If the child wants more information, you could say, "father starts the baby growing in mother's body. Many tiny sperm cells come from the father's body. One sperm cell joins with one egg cell in mother's body. When the two cells join they start to grow into a baby."

Then comes the question most parents find hardest: "How does Father's cell get into Mother's body?" or "How did Daddy put the cell in you?" Once again, keep it simple: "father's cells come from his penis. It fits into mother's vagina." Around this time, you could explain that the cells are made in the testicles, and that they come out in a fluid called semen. Be careful to emphasize that this fluid is different from urine, and explain to your son that he won't have any semen until around the time he becomes a grownup.

Don't be alarmed if your child bursts out

laughing, or refuses to believe you at first. Your straightforward answers will still stand you in good stead when he comes back for more information. Children often ask the same questions about sex over and over again. Sometimes this is because they have simply forgotten the answer. Other times, it may be because they have sensed a certain hesitation in your answers. Usually it only means that they need time to understand all the related pieces of information they are gradually collecting. This is true of many questions a child asks about various subjects.

Each child will probably ask further questions in his own particular way. Many children want to know: "How did I eat when I was inside you?" "Where was I before I was growing in you?" "Does it take years and years for a baby to grow?" "Why doesn't the mother's cell go into the father?" Other questions—"When do you and Daddy make babies?" "Did you and Daddy like doing that?"—may give you a chance to explain that love-making is a thoroughly

From Two to Five

From two to five years a child develops markedly, gaining the ability to communicate, respond, and master new skills. Each child's rate of development differs, of course, but here are some examples of the average behavior you can expect.

Approximate Age	Activity	Vocal Reactions	Social Reactions
2 years	Runs well with good co-ordination	Good vocabulary	Watches other children; plays by them rather than with them
	Builds towers of four to eight blocks	Starts to make small sentences of two and three words	
	Carries out directions well	Starts to use such pronouns as "I" and "me"	Loves rough and tumble play
	Loves looking at books and enjoys rhythm		
3 years	Uses larger blocks and makes more intricate buildings	Usually speaks very well and has a good vocabulary	Joins other boys and girls in play
		Uses plurals and pronouns	Is generally cooperative
	Enjoys playing with toy trucks, fire engines, airplanes, dolls and doll carriages	Knows own sex	Willing to take turns
		Knows full name	Will help setting the table
	Will do simple cutout puzzles	Knows songs and some rhymes	
	Loves swings, slides, climbing ladders	Constantly asks questions	
		Repeats three numbers or a sentence of six syllables	
	Uses crayons more effectively and is beginning to enjoy finger paints		
	Dresses and undresses self, but usually needs help with buttons		
	Washes and dries hands and face		

enjoyable, but private, activity, and that mother and father do it because they love each other, and want to have a baby to love.

As always in talking with your child, how you give this kind of information is as important as what you say. A child will quickly sense how you feel about discussing sex. If you are prepared for his questions, and can answer them in a relaxed, matter-of-fact way, he will feel comfortable about bringing further questions to you as the years go by. Reading a few books on sex education written for children—and even repeating certain "loaded" words over to themselves—has helped many mothers present the information comfortably when the time comes. It is certainly a good idea to get a book about sex written for the age level of your child to read aloud and look at together when giving your explanations.

Of course, we are busy communicating attitudes about sex to our children from the time they are born. The way in which a baby is cuddled, touched, held, and cared

Approximate Age	Activity	Vocal Reactions	Social Reactions
4 years	Throws ball fairly well Brushes teeth Often pretends he is an animal in his imaginative play Hops on one foot Uses scissors to cut out pictures Climbs well	Obeys commands fairly well when told to place something "on" or "under" or "on the side" Knows one or more colors correctly Loves to sing and dance Immense enjoyment of phonograph records Tells a story Counts four objects	Very social Enjoys playmates and play group Frequently quotes his mother and father as authorities At times may be very bossy Occasionally has imaginary playmates Goes to toilet alone
5 years	Generally well organized Can throw a ball well, rides well on his tricycle, and can walk a straight line with ease Can lace his shoes with ease, and sews through holes in a card Enjoys drawing and painting An excellent blockbuilder as a rule; prefers using large blocks Enjoys copying letters and numbers Enjoys routines Skips	Listens to his phonograph records, and plays them over and over Sings many songs and nursery rhymes Often sings with his records or with TV and radio programs Names four colors Counts ten objects	Enjoys helping prepare for parties and other occasions Plays well with other children Loves rhythms and dancing, and group singing Will play housekeeping with other children Enjoys pretending he is an adult Likes to run short errands Dresses and undresses unaided

for gives him his first vital experience of love, and the pleasure of physical contact. When you bathe or feed your baby, dress or toilet train your child, your attitudes toward his body teach him as much about sex as when you answer his specific questions. Ill-concealed distaste at changing diapers, or at a child's proud performance on the potty, a slap or scolding when he examines his sex organs, or inquires how Grandpa goes to the bathroom, communicate to a child that certain parts of the body are nasty or shameful, and certain talk is taboo.

Another aspect of a three- to five-year old's development that may worry parents is his attachment to the parent of the opposite sex. "Mommy, when I grow up, I'm going to marry you," said her son Mack, age four. "What about Daddy?" said his mother. "Oh, he'll be dead." Little girls often speak to their fathers in the same way. Unless parents are aware of what this attitude means, they can feel needlessly anxious and rejected. This is a child's first experiment with his maleness (or femaleness)—a safe testing ground for future relationships with the opposite sex. If handled wisely, it provides a sound basis for mature attachments later.

Despite any jealousy or resentment one parent may feel during this stage, it doesn't help to taunt or criticize the child, to label him a "sissy" or her "a real Daddy's girl". We can best help our child, and ourselves, through this period by accepting it as a normal phase in development, and by continuing to be affectionate to one another, and to the child, without letting him come between us. He needs to be reassured that both his parents love him, and we can tell him that when he grows up he will find someone of his own age to love and marry. Gradually, as the child enters the school years, he will drop his strong emotional attachment to the parent of the opposite sex, and begin to model himself on the parent of the same sex.

If we find it hard to talk to our children about sex, we generally find it a great deal harder to answer their questions about

The pronounced preference of a four-year-old for the parent of the opposite sex should not be a source of jealousy, although it's not always easy to accept. It's a natural stage in a child's development of sexual awareness, and will soon change.

death. "Is he dead?" a child may ask suddenly one day when watching TV. "What does 'died' mean?" "What happens when you die?" "Why did Grandpa die? Doesn't he love me any more?" "Why can't the doctor fix him up again?" "Why don't you make him come back?" "Where is Grandpa now?" "Can he see me where he is?" "When are you going to die, Mommy?"

What you tell your child about death will, of course, depend not only on your own attitudes and beliefs, but also on your sensitive knowledge of your child's personality. Only by listening carefully to the kind of questions a child asks can we detect particular anxieties that may lie behind them. Four-year-old Amanda, for example, having been told that people who die go to a nice place called heaven, was only interested in practical details at first. "Do they take their pyjamas with them?" she wanted to know, and, "Can they watch television there?" A little later, however, she announced tearfully, "I don't want to die, Mommy." This was the start of many anxious questions about death: "Will I die?" "P'raps I won't die if I'm good, will I?" "Will Uncle Peter

die when he goes to the hospital?" Another child, after being told of the death of an elderly aunt, continually asked whether her grandparents were still there, and if she would ever see them again. Then she began asking how old her parents and other family members were. She was worrying about the connection of age and death.

Sometimes a child's fears are less easily detected. Three-and-a-half year old Louis, for instance, was deeply distressed by the death of his grandmother. Time and again he asked his mother questions about how and why people die. Although she did her best to answer him truthfully, he kept begging her to "bring Grandma back." It was not until nearly a year later that his mother finally understood the real reason for his distress. "It was my fault!" Louis suddenly blurted out. "It was my fault

The death of a pet is
as hard to explain as
any death, but may give
you the opening to talk
about it in terms a
child might grasp. The
important thing is to
try to understand your
child's special fears,
and to make your ex-
planation deal with them
as much as you can.

Children over the age of about two to three are not too young to understand something about death. The trouble is that what they understand is likely to be a highly confused interpretation of what has really happened. Unless we help a child to understand the true facts, he may well believe that he was somehow to blame for the death, that he, too, may die for some supposed misdeed, or that he may suddenly be left alone with no one to love and care for him. We need to be on the alert for any questions that hint at such fears so that we can do our best to dispel them.

Some suggestions for answering your child's questions about death appear in the Question & Answer section of this book. It is important to remember, however, that no single explanation of death is right for every child. Whatever our answers, we cannot hope to spare our child from all anxiety about an event that we ourselves find so painfully hard to accept. Provided we try to be as honest and reassuring as we can, and remain sensitive to any ill-founded fears the child may have, we can help him to cope with this most distressing of all facts of life.

One of the reasons why a young child may be particularly distressed, or even blame himself for the death of someone close to him is his belief in the magical power of words and wishes. To a child under six, it seems that words, and the thoughts that go with them, can actually make things happen. Even as adults we don't entirely lose this feeling. "Everything's going wonderfully— touch wood," we say. Or, "I can't tell you about it now, just in case it doesn't happen." In a young child the fear that words or

'cause I made a noise when she was sick, and Grandpa was angry." Susan, on the other hand, was spared the news of her aunt's death. Her parents thought her "too young to understand" at age three, and simply told her that Aunt Ruth had "gone away." Every time Susan asked when her aunt would come back, she was told, "some day." Then one day Susan said abruptly, "Aunt Ruth's dead, isn't she? And you'll die, too."

59

feelings can affect events is much more powerful. If Stephen yells at his brother, "I hate you, you're a stinker, I wish you'd never come back!" he may live in terror that something really will happen to his brother—and it will be his fault because he wished something bad would happen.

A preschooler is busy coming to terms with the difficult fact that human beings have bad feelings as well as good ones, that they can hate as well as love. When your child shouts, "I hate you! I'll kill you!" "You're mean and horrid. I wish I had another Mommy!" you are likely to feel hurt and shocked. It can take a lot of self-restraint not to reply, "Tommy, how could you!" "That's a dreadful thing to say to your mother!" "Don't you dare talk to me like that again!" What effect do such words have on the child? It tells him that he must never feel anger toward his parents, and that we cannot accept his having hostile as

well as loving feelings. By increasing his guilt about such feelings, we make it harder for him to come to terms with them. If, on the other hand, we can acknowledge his present rage by saying, "I know you're mad at me. You hate me right now, but you'll feel differently later," we show that we understand how he feels, we recognize that people do have angry feelings, but that this does not alter or destroy their other, more loving feelings. By helping him to cope

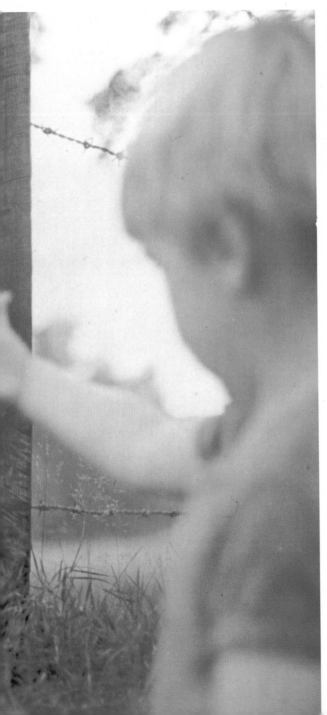

The makings of a nightmare are in many of a child's ordinary daily experiences. That huge bull may seem merely big and lumbering by day—but it could become an enemy in the boy's dreams. Friendly looking monsters in a book might be amusing, but who knows whether they might not turn into foes during sleep?

with the hating part of himself, we are helping him to grow and mature.

While a child is learning to control his feelings, or to express them in acceptable ways, he may sometimes seek an outlet by transferring angry or aggressive impulses to things outside of himself. A child's fears of animals, insects, big machines, thunder, or darkness are often a projection of his anxieties about the dangers of his own feelings. When a child panics at the sight of a dog, refuses to walk under a bridge, or wakes screaming in the dark, our immediate instinct is, of course, to reassure him. "There's nothing to be afraid of," we say. But to the child, there *is* something to be afraid of. To him, that dog is terrifying, and the monster he sees at the foot of his bed is real. We need to accept his fear if we are to help him through it. Rather than saying, "There's no need to be frightened," we can encourage him to talk about his anxiety: "That dog's scary, isn't he? What makes him so scary?" "Tell me about the monster. What's he like?"

The fears and anxieties of a child's waking life take on even more horrifying proportions in a bad dream. A nightmare is as real to the child as if it had actually happened, and is a terrifying experience. When your child is frightened by a dream, he needs your sympathetic understanding of his fears. Holding and soothing him, staying with him till he falls asleep, leaving the light on if he wants it, all this will help. But talking with him gently about the dream may also bring him relief and comfort, and may sometimes reveal the true source of his anxieties.

Even the healthiest child from the most loving family is apt to have occasional nightmares, and apparently irrational fears. This can be very upsetting and worrying to parents, but it will pass. There are ways in which we can help. We need to remember that to a young child many things are strange and frightening. He is very small, and often feels powerless in contrast to the big, strong adults around him. If we discipline our children with warmth and sincere concern, they need not be so afraid of our power. If we use that power to guide the child, to help him grow and mature, then our greater strength will be seen by him as good, and generally beneficial. There will still be plenty of times when a child will see his parents' authority as an interference, and will resent them. But when parents are generally helpful, the child will be less frightened of their strength or anger, and this can lessen his tendency· toward fears and bad dreams.

Play, too, allows a child to discharge some of the fears and anxieties that build up. He needs to have an opportunity to play at being mommy or daddy, and to scold his

toys, his brothers and sisters, or his parents as part of a game. He may want a collection of toy trucks and cars that zoom around, crash, and make a lot of noise. He may like to play at being Zorro or Bat Man. It is exciting for a child to use his energy this way, and we need to allow him a certain amount of running around, screeching, and booming. Let your child play at being a horse, a lion, or a barking, biting dog—it's a way for him

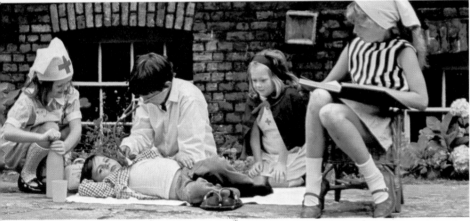

Play is not only fun, but is also a necessary outlet for children. Through play they can let out some of their fears and aggressions, and also give full expression to their fantasies and imaginations. Pretending to be doctors, nurses, cowboys or Indians; wandering among flowers; fondling a pet mouse—all are part of healthful and enjoyable playtime.

to let out aggression. If a child is allowed to do this in a playful way, such feelings are less apt to be expressed in harmful behavior, or through fears and nightmares.

You can often learn a lot about your child's inner feelings as he "acts them out" in play, but it is best not to intervene. Understanding a child's feelings, and giving him help when he needs it, is one thing, but even a four-year-old has a right to the privacy of his innermost thoughts. Play can, however, help us in a different way. Through games we can prepare a child for a visit to the doctor, the arrival of a new babysitter, a family vacation, or mother's going to the hospital. By acting out such changes in the child's life, and discussing them openly ahead of time, we can help him cope with difficult situations or important changes, and prepare him for the next big step in his life—going to school.

Going to School

4

It was David's first day at school, and his mother was close to tears. "It isn't that he made a fuss," she said. "In fact, he went trotting into the classroom without even looking back. It was just that I suddenly realized how much I was going to miss him."

Most of us have mixed feelings when our child first starts school. Mingled with pride at his growing independence, and relief at having a bit more time to ourselves, is a certain sadness that a whole stage in our child's life is over. We wonder how he will adjust to his new experience, and how it will affect our relationship with him. We may fear that other people—teachers and children —will now take our place as the most important influence in his life. What will the teacher think of our child? Will she see that Phil is naturally slow to warm up to new things, but is fine once encouraged? Will she recognize that Crystal is a high-spirited, creative child who needs plenty of scope? Will she find fault with our child, and will we, as parents, be judged and found wanting?

Whether they begin in nursery school or kindergarten, most children are eager to start school. This is a big moment in their lives, a milestone in growing up, that they have probably talked and dreamed of for months beforehand. Even so, it generally takes a child some time to settle in. For the first four or five weeks almost all children show some signs of emotional strain. Doing without mother can be difficult, and even a child who is managing well at school may need extra cuddling and signs of affection at home. Some children return to more babyish ways, burst into tears easily, begin bed-wetting again, or become generally

Going to school is a big step toward growing up. Even if they have a hard first day and a few trying weeks, children generally settle in happily before very long.

64

Some children find being away from the protected home environment almost unbearable at first; some immediately take to the new life with unabated joy; most will finally relax and take their place with other children and teacher. It will depend a lot on how independent and secure your child feels.

cranky and difficult. Others may say disappointingly little about their activities at school, and seem to find it easier to adjust by keeping their school and home life strictly separate. So long as we are tolerant and understanding at this time, listening to the child if he does want to talk over his feelings about school, and being just as loving toward him as before, symptoms of tension should soon pass. If they persist after the first few weeks, it is wise to talk the problem over with your child's teacher.

Both you and your child will get off to a happier start if you have done your pre-school homework. Most of us take a great deal of trouble to prepare our child for starting school, but sometimes we may try to be too encouraging. Peter's parents, for example, told him that school was a wonderful place where he would learn to read and write like his big sister, and would soon become as clever as Mommy and Daddy. But after the first few days, Peter seemed very dejected. When his father started to read him his usual bedtime story, he burst into tears. "I want to read it myself, and I can't," he wept. He had believed that going to school meant he would be able to read right away. Jill's parents, on the other hand, stressed how much fun she would have on her first day at school, with exciting new things to do all day, and lots of nice children to play with. All went well. Jill declared that school was "O.K." But the next morning when mother announced "time for school," she looked dismayed. "D'you mean I have to go *again*?" she said.

While we want to make going to school sound attractive, it is better to stick to facts about what the child will find there so that he can build up a realistic picture. We can tell him exactly when he will go to school, the kind of things he will do, the things that might happen—like what to do if he wants to go to the toilet—and when we will come and pick him up. If we make school sound like too much fun, and something disconcerting happens, the child may be so disappointed that he finds it hard to adjust

67

Is your child often the first with the answer? You'll want to be careful not to pressure him too much for continually high grades. Is he rather the type who has to work hard to keep up? You'll want to praise him for what he is able to do, and let him know you accept him as he is.

to the real situation. Rather than saying how wonderful school will be, we can explain that he may feel a little lonely at first, and that some children may cry when their mommies leave, but that the teacher will help him, and that we will be back to meet him later.

The best preparation of all is for your child to visit the school with you ahead of time—more than once if possible—and to meet his teacher. Many schools make arrangements for this, and it is an ideal opportunity to show your child which door he will go in,

where he will hang his coat, where the toilets are, and so on. A school visit can also help you visualize some of the practical details of his day. By knowing for yourself what his school is like, you can answer his questions more accurately, and avoid passing on feelings colored by your own school experiences.

Some first day fears are only natural, but what if, despite all your careful preparation, your kindergartner dissolves into a trantrum at the door, or clings sobbing to your side, and refuses to let you go? Some children find it especially hard to part from their parents. They may have had little chance to practice their independence up till now, or simply not be quite ready for school. Stresses at home, such as the arrival of a new baby or friction between parents, can make a child particularly anxious about leaving his mother's side. Sometimes, too, a mother's own anxiety about her child's readiness for school, or her reluctance to part with him, communicates itself to the child.

Whatever the reason, teachers are generally experienced in managing this situation, and will often suggest that a mother stay with her child at first. If this happens, it would be unkind to try to slip away while your child's attention is elsewhere—a ruse he'll spot in seconds. Better to stay for as long as need be, until he seems to have settled in well. Occasionally a child who is not mature enough for school may continue to be thoroughly miserable even after a week or two, and, in this case, a pediatrician might be helpful in suggesting ways to develop his confidence. Chances are, however, that your child will be like Barry who,

Your child's happy adjustment to school will probably bring a need for adjustment to you when he or she starts quoting the teacher as the highest authority on everything. It's important that parent and teacher respect and support each other in filling their roles in a child's life. You needn't be worried that you will come second in love to teacher.

after the first couple of days that his mother stayed, turned to her and demanded, "Why are you still here?"

Once your child has adjusted happily to school, you soon become aware of the other adult who has entered his life. If there is one thing that is guaranteed to infuriate parents of a schoolage child, it is those sentences that begin, "My teacher says . . ." Any normal, devoted parent is likely to feel a sneaking jealousy when Miss Jones is endlessly quoted as the leading authority on everything from polar icecaps to good table manners. Fathers seethe as their ideas are apparently dismissed in favor of teacher's, and mothers resent being addressed absent-mindedly as "Miss Jones." (The fact that Miss Jones hears a great deal about "my Mommy and Daddy" and is sometimes called "Mommy" by mistake may be scant consolation.) However, it is wise to swallow your annoyance, and support the teacher's statement as gracefully as you can at this stage. First graders generally regard their teacher with awe—only later will she shed her halo—and they want her approval.

The teacher, in turn, needs to establish a friendly and trusting relationship with the child if she is to teach him successfully. But, for the child, his parents' love and approval still come first. Home continues to be the most important place in his life—a haven of warmth and comfort against the new pressures he is facing, and a secure background for his continuing emotional growth. When home and school are in conflict, when a child is told, "That's ridiculous. What can Miss Jones be thinking of?", or 'I'll have to see your Miss Jones. I won't have her treat

you like this," he begins to lose faith in his teacher, and finds it hard to accept and learn from her. Rather than competing for his loyalties, both parent and teacher need to respect and support each other's role in the child's life.

As time goes on, there are bound to be occasions when you need to consult the teacher about some aspect of your child's development away from home. Is Maureen ready to move from kindergarten to first grade although she is not quite six? The teacher says Greg might do better if he were held back in first grade. Is she right? Why has Sybil suddenly stopped wanting to go to school? Why does the teacher think that Elaine is "smart but lazy?" Most of us approach interviews with our child's teacher in some trepidation. She, in turn, may not feel any too comfortable about meeting us. However, it is important to try to bridge the parent-teacher gap if we want to find the best ways of helping our child.

The teacher feels that Joey is inattentive, and behaves badly in class. Rather than rushing to Joey's defense, can you help her understand any possible reasons for his apparent misbehavior? Is he a highly active child who finds it hard to sit still for long? Maybe the teacher could let him help around the class to give him an outlet for his restlessness. Is he a child whose shyness could be mistaken for lack of interest? A little gentle encouragement might be what he needs. Is he undergoing a period of tension at starting a new grade? Are there problems at home that could be making him anxious? Knowing about these will help the teacher to be more sympathetic. One

Experiment A
We want to find out
 dirty hands are
using green water.
Some of us think
e water will stay
ean if no dirty hands
e put in the water
April 26

Exper
We want t
it dead anima
causing gree

Some t
no dea
tank, th
clean
Apri

Experime
We want to
it plants are
water
Some think
are

Liquid
1. starch
2. motor oil
3. glycerine
4. water
5. pink nail polish
6. orange juice-frozen
7. orange juice-jar
8. pear juice
9. wine
10. milk
11. dill pickle juice
12. cough syrup
13. lemon juice-bottle
14. detergent

teacher, for instance, hearing that a youngster was worried about the arrival of a new baby in the family, encouraged her pupils to tell the class about their baby brothers or sisters. These "share-and-tell" sessions were such a success that several children, unable to join in, went home and begged their mothers to have another baby!

Being as open-minded as you can about your child's behavior, at home and at school, and sharing ideas and information about his personality and his weaknesses, as well as his strengths, pays dividends in terms of his intellectual development, and his emotional health. You will want to ask questions about your child's schoolwork, too, of course. Why isn't Jane getting such

good grades this year? Why can't Mickey read yet? Can the teacher give you some idea of what could be causing the trouble? Is there anything you can do to help? Keep on asking until you find a satisfactory answer. Explanations such as, "I'm afraid she's rather lazy," "He just doesn't work hard enough," "She could do better if she tried," don't explain anything. Can you and the teacher work together to find out *why* Jane is lazy or *why* Mickey doesn't try? If you cannot diagnose the problem together, maybe the school's guidance counselor, or your own pediatrician could help. Meanwhile, if your child is having a hard time at school, let him know that you realize it's tough, and you sympathize. You may need to be firm

You can do a great deal to foster a love of learning and experimentation in your child outside of school. Visits to museums, or help with hobbies will broaden his interests, and make learning fun.

in explaining why he must go to school, but you can make sure he gets lots of good experiences at home.

Home experiences are also vital in fostering a child's enthusiasm for learning. The stories you read aloud, and the trips you make to the library increase his interest in books— and so does your obvious enjoyment of reading. Your interest in a wide variety of topics, and your readiness to try to answer his questions, encourage him to seek out information for himself. Family excursions, visits to the zoo, to the airport, to public buildings, to the countryside or other towns, add to your child's store of knowledge, and stimulate his desire to learn more. Crafts and hobbies, tools of his own, a chance to

help Dad out in his workshop, all open the way for experimentation and discovery. Discussing a TV program, or sharing in family conversations increase fluency and confidence in expressing ideas. When we encourage a child to talk about what he has seen and done, and how he felt, and when we listen with interest to his ideas and feelings, we not only keep the lines of communication open between us, but we also contribute to his intellectual growth.

There are many other ways in which we can play a part in our child's life at school. Parent-teacher meetings and discussion groups are invaluable for learning about the school's methods and problems, and for talking over any special worries with other concerned parents. Even a child who is reluctant to talk about school likes to know that his parents are interested in its activities, and consider them important. How we react to the work he brings home is important too. Can we praise him for the nine arithmetic problems he got right, rather than worrying him about the one that's wrong? Can we admire that whole line of well-formed letters instead of asking why all the "E's" are back-to-front?

Of course we are interested in his scrapbooks and drawings, and we want to be generous with our praise. But even well-intentioned comments can misfire. "Aren't you clever!" can dash the confidence of a six-year-old who is beginning to realize that there are at least half-a-dozen children in his class who are smarter than he is. "That's a good drawing. I like it," would be more honest and more helpful.

"What is it?" "Yes, honey, very nice. But why did you paint everything blue?" "Shouldn't your house have windows? Here, let me show you." These words can sound like, "Your painting isn't good enough. Paintings have to represent something. There is a 'right' way of doing them." Self-expression is far more important than accuracy. By saying, "What a colorful picture. Does it have a story and would you like to tell me about it?" we can encourage a child to talk about the feelings that went into his work. By pinning his pictures on the wall, a family bulletin board, or even the door of a kitchen cabinet, we make him feel important and eager to experiment some more.

The schoolage child is beginning to feel the pressures of competition, and to make comparisons between himself and other children. It doesn't take a child long to notice that George can run faster than he, that Skip is stronger, or that Kate can always answer the teacher's questions. Pressure from his peers is tough enough without our joining in. Children need continuing proof that we love and value them for themselves, whether they win or lose. What they don't need is for us to say, "If your

The first grader has a growing interest in all kinds of things—plants, toys that can be operated, reading, pets, and television, especially action programs; but he hardly ever sits still for a minute. He needs many expressions of approval to help him settle into good behavior.

sister can get good grades, so can you;" "No, you dope, not like that. Watch how Dick does it;" "Come along now. Boys your age don't cry;" "If only Margie were more like her brother!" Remarks like these, heard or overheard, strike at a child's self-respect, and make him feel inadequate. Children need our support, which may even be in the form of a gentle nudge from time to time. Above all, they need our belief in their right to be themselves.

This is never more true than within the family itself. What parent hasn't heard a plaintive: "It's not fair!" "How come Billy gets to stay up later than me?" "You're always fussing over her." "You never have time for me." "You let Ned do everything!" "You don't love me!"

Jealousy is part and parcel of family living. Each child wants to be his parents' favorite, the best loved one. Telling a child that you love him and his sister equally is about as comforting as if your husband said he loved you as much as an old flame. Jealousy, as we know from our own experience, doesn't respond to reason. Denying a child's feelings ("That's silly! You get just as many privileges as Billy and you know it.") only makes him feel worse. We need to accept that our children do feel jealous sometimes, and we shouldn't be afraid to sympathize with them. While we cannot hope to eliminate jealousy altogether, we can ensure that we haven't slipped into the habit of favoring one child in particular, that we respect each child's individuality, and spend time helping each one to develop his own special talents. When we reinforce each child's sense of being cherished as a person in his own right, he can feel secure enough to share our love—most of the time. Family rivalry has this in its favor at least. Handled tactfully, it can help a child to learn some valuable lessons in the art of getting along with others.

From the age of six or seven onward, a child is busy learning other lessons, too: about honesty, about cheating, stealing, lying, being cruel, about the difference between right and wrong. It is not uncommon for six-to-nine's to steal from home once or twice, or to come home with something that does not belong to them. Parents who discover that their child has been stealing are naturally horrified. But before we explode into angry accusations, or worry ourselves sick that we are raising a delinquent, we need to understand some of the reasons why children steal.

A young child does not yet have a strong sense of ownership. For years he has been encouraged to share his possessions generously with his playmates, and he may see nothing wrong in "borrowing" things that belong to others. Sometimes stealing comes from a need for friendship. A lonely child may steal candy and gum (or the money for it) to buy acceptance from others. Stealing may be a cry for help, when a child is undergoing tensions at home or at school, or when he longs for more affection. A child who is unable to find an outlet for hostile feelings may steal from his parents as a way to express his anger. An older child may, of course, steal because he has been egged on by his peers who regard taking things from stores and shops as a "dare".

How, then, should we react when we

Left: a good atmosphere at home, and close family feelings help children to adjust more easily to the situations they'll have to face in life—including school.

Right: even in families that get on well there are bound to be spats between children (as well as parents). The general good feeling of love and understanding will overcome these temporary clashes.

discover that our child has stolen something? Experts agree that a firm statement is wiser than lengthy sermons or harsh punishments. "Did you steal that doll?" or "Why did you take that money?" will probably cause a child to lie in self-defense. When you are certain that your child has taken something, suggests child psychologist Dr. Haim Ginott, it is best to say simply, "That doll doesn't belong to you. Give it back." "The candy bar belongs to the store. Put it back on the shelf," or "You took a dollar from my pocketbook. Please return it."

Rather than labeling a child a thief, stopping his pocket money, or threatening, "You'll end up in jail if you go on like this," we can tell him that we are disappointed in his behavior, and we can help him make restitution without humiliation. For the child who occasionally gives in to temptation, our disapproval can be punishment enough. While we need to be alert to possible reasons for stealing (does the child need help in making friends or are we not giving him enough signs of affection?), an isolated theft is rarely cause for alarm. It is when stealing is persistent that we need to seek help in finding out why.

Another problem for parents is lying. Most of us are familiar with the highly colored stories of six-to-nine-year-olds. "Gene shot a huge bear in the woods today." "I saw a man flying in the sky." "Sandra's Mommy gives her an enormous candy bar every night." "My Dad's got a million dollars—so there!" A child may dream up tall tales to draw attention to himself, but more often than not, such fantasy lies are simply an

expression of his vivid imagination. If we listen to them we can often learn about his feelings and wishes. Rather than reacting with a, "Don't be silly, honey. You know that's not true," a sarcastic, "Really? And I suppose he shot an elephant, too," or a bored "So what," we can provide creative outlets for a child's fancies. By emphasizing that these are "pretend" stories ("Wouldn't it be fun if a man could fly! Would he have wings, do you think, or just flap his arms?" "Let's pretend we did meet a bear. What would we do?") we can turn storytelling into a game. That way, we encourage creativity while still allowing the child to draw comfort from make-believe.

While most of us can overlook the occasional transparent whopper, we do worry about the lies children tell to get themselves out of trouble. When children tell this kind of lie it is because they feel that lying is somehow safer than telling the truth. If mother rages, "Did you or did you not break that vase?" it may seem much safer to Jane to insist that she didn't. No matter that mother saw her do it. All she knows is that she doesn't like to be yelled at, and she is scared of the punishment she may receive. Her concern is to win back her mother's favor, and she is too frightened to understand that her lying is simply making mother angrier than ever.

Accusations, interrogations, and harsh punishments only make a child more fearful. He needs to know that we recognize that people sometimes make mistakes, and that it is safe to admit wrongdoings. This doesn't mean that the child should not be made aware of the consequences of his behavior. If he breaks something he should help to fix it, or to clean up the mess. That way, he has a sense of usefulness, and can feel that he is making some amends. If he is allowed to be helpful, and is praised for telling the truth even though he has misbehaved, he will learn that honesty can indeed be the best policy.

Sometimes children lie because their parents' expectations are too high. A child who feels that his parents' approval depends on his success may try to hide the fact that he is getting poor grades in school. Other times, children may lie because the truth is too painful for them. A child whose mother is very ill may tell all kinds of stories to his friends. He may brag about the places she takes him, and the things she does for him. He tells these "lies" because he can't bear to face the truth. He doesn't want to believe that his mother is ill, and cannot do the things that he would like for him. We need to recognize times of great stress in a child's life, and to treat his "lies" or stories with compassion. Rather than scolding him for his behavior, we can give him the comfort and help he needs to cope with painful situations such as illness, death, or the splitting up of the family. We can recognize that he is feeling bad, and show him that we understand. No child needs to be told to "act like a man," or that "big boys don't cry". He may be able to pretend to his parents that he is not upset, but all the pretending in the world won't change his true feelings.

In general, when we are prepared to accept our child's feelings, we encourage him to communicate openly and honestly with us. But that means accepting resentful feelings as well as loving ones. If Marlene gets spanked for saying she'd like to get rid of her sister, and is made to say she didn't mean it, she may decide that mother likes her better when she hides the truth.

We often forget that, while demanding high standards of honesty from our children, we allow ourselves "little white lies" or half-truths—and they know it. What about

Being over stern and over strict when you think your child has told a lie can often make him stick to it more desperately out of fear of severe punishment. When your boy or girl has done something wrong, how much better to help them own up to it by your understanding attitude, and willingness to consider their side. Of course, you can—and should —expect them to make retribution when possible.

that promise to visit Aunt Marjorie that we keep putting off? What about our mumbled excuse to an unwanted caller that we were "just going out", or admiring a neighbor's new sofa when only last night we were telling Daddy how ugly it was? We teach our children most about honesty when we are honest ourselves.

That's all very well, you might say, but we have to be tactful sometimes. Explaining the delicate distinction between tact and truth to a literal-minded child isn't easy.

We can, however, emphasize the need to be kind to other people, and point out the effect that thoughtless words or actions can have on them. We can explain that some remarks can hurt a person's feelings and make them unhappy, so we try not to say them. When we respect a child's own feelings, and try to be kind and considerate ourselves, he will gradually learn to follow our example and show respect for others himself.

Whatever the values and attitudes we want to impart to our children, it is always our example that counts in the end. Do you teach politeness by continually prodding Ginny to say "thank you", or by never failing to say "thank you" yourself? Do you teach respect by telling Daniel how rude he is to interrupt, or by promising him his turn to talk, and listening when he does? Do you persuade Tim to be thoughtful by nagging him to pick up his toys, or by offering to help him sometimes? If we hope to convince our children, we have to try to practice what we preach to them.

Growing Up

5

Nine-to-twelve's are unexpectedly mature and childish by turn. They are also extremely shy of the opposite sex—the boys usually pursuing their traditional games, the girls beginning to imitate Mommy.

Pete and Andy are up the street building a hideout with their gang. Bobby is busy painting a sign for his bedroom door. "Private. No trespassing," it reads. "Keep out—this means YOU!" Gerry is taking his transistor to pieces, while his mother cleans out the goldfish bowl, and feeds the two fish he seems to have forgotten. Margaret is begging her father for a camera "like all the other kids." Sandra wants a puppy: "I'll take care of him, Mommy. You won't need

to do anything, I promise." Bonnie drifts through the living room, book in hand, pretending to be Mary, Queen of Scots. In a moment the whole house is in an uproar as she trips over her brother's marbles.

Nine-to-twelve's are busy developing their sense of self. The drive for separateness, just emerging at age two, has moved into a higher gear. When you long to impose some order on your youngster's happy confusion, when you resent having to knock at Bobby's

The companionship and approval of his best friend is one of the most important things in life to a preteener. Through such friendship, a child gets support he needs to work toward full independence.

door, when you're tempted to take a peep at Bonnie's diary or nag Gerry about the forgotten goldfish, it helps to remember what all these things mean to your child. They are his ways of finding out about himself, about who he is, what interests him, and what he, as an individual can do. Out of that clutter of pebbles and shells, old playing cards, rusty bottle caps, dried flowers, horse pictures, model airplane parts, matchbooks, and other stuff, your youngster is evolving a sense of his own identity.

Brimming over with self-confidence one minute, and amazingly childish the next, a 9-to-12-year-old is growing up, three steps forward, and one step back fashion. He needs the chance to practice independence, but he also needs to be able to retreat to the comfort and security of home when the going

gets tough. Even though he can sometimes appear so self-sufficient, it would be a mistake to expect too much of him now, instead of continuing to listen, encourage, and help him with his problems. Sloppy, noisy, and unpredictable he may be, infuriating when he "doesn't hear" what you say or "forgets" what you asked, but a 9-to-12-year-old can also be one of the world's most spontaneous, idealistic, and sensitive creatures.

During these years, however, it may seem that your child's first allegiance is to his peers. Most of all he wants to belong to a group, to be the same as the other kids, to dress, talk, look, and behave like the rest of the gang. Once again, we may begin to feel a little displaced as group values, or the opinions of one or two close pals seem to dominate our youngster's life. However, a

wise parent tries to realize what this loyalty to his age group means in terms of a child's development. The group can give him the support he needs as he works his way toward greater independence. Group rituals, rhymes and chants, secret passwords, and "in" talk weld the group together, and help a child to feel secure. Now, too, he is practicing ways of relating to others, and learning what it is like to live in society.

This is the positive side of childhood friendships and gangs. But there may be another side, too. What if your child's gang seems to be teaching him unacceptable ways of behaving? Supposing your youngster chooses a friend whom you consider to be a completely bad influence?

First of all we need to recognize that a child's choice of friends usually answers some emotional need. A normally well-behaved child, for example, may sometimes be drawn to unruly friends because they express aggressive feelings he dare not acknowledge in himself. Other times, children may choose companions whose personalities complement their own. A shy child may prefer an out-going playmate, or a dreamy child a more down-to-earth pal. These relationships can be mutually beneficial, with each child gaining something from his counterpart. Even negative friendships may have something to offer a child. Mixing with various types of children, learning about the differences between people, and finding out for himself about their strengths and weaknesses contribute to the development of a child's own personality.

It isn't always so easy, however. Children's friendships can sometimes be mutually harmful, too: the bossy child whose meek friend always falls in with his wishes, the bully who finds an ever-willing victim, or the aggressive pair who seem to spark each other off. Maybe your child will cling to a friendship with a seriously unmanageable playmate, who really does seem to bring out the worst in him. In situations like these, we may well feel that we must intervene, and take steps to discourage the relationship.

How, then, do you go about ending a friendship that you consider harmful to your child? Criticism of the chosen friend rarely helps. A child's friendships mean a great deal to him, and he will probably resent what you say as an attack on him for choosing such a pal. Forbidding the friendship is usually just as unsuccessful. Better to take a more positive approach and try, as subtly as you can, to help your child cultivate other friendships. Can you find another friend—someone your child likes, or at least tolerates—and map out some fun things for the two of them to do for the day? How about letting them see a good movie, take a ferryboat ride, or go on a trip to the Natural History Museum, with plans for a delicious ice cream soda or banana split afterward?

Henry's parents found that their son wasn't

half so eager to dash over to his friend's when Dad arranged to spend more time with him. Father and son had a regular date to play checkers after Henry had finished his homework, and go to a ball game with a couple of neighbors every Saturday. Another couple encouraged their youngster to join the Cub Scouts, which supplied him with plenty of approved outlets for adventure, and introduced him to some new friends. Mrs. P., on the other hand, decided to invite her daughter Sue's unsuitable friend over with several other girls. "I felt that by giving Sue's friend an example of how kids can behave nicely and still have fun, I might win her over," explains Mrs. P. "I also found it helped for Sue to see this particular friend in relation to other girls."

Mrs. P.'s method doesn't always turn the

It's a boisterous and active age between nine and the teens, especially for boys. They're off and away—usually with the gang—to take a fast whirl around at the playground, to scramble down the hill, or to go bike riding. Boys of this age seem to live for the approval of their peers—even though competition with their friends can sometimes create problems.

trick, of course, and it may seem a little cruel to have to prise your youngster, however gently, away from friendship with a "problem child." Maybe you can see reasons why this child is disturbed (a broken or breaking home, an alcoholic parent, an abusive older brother, for example) and feel that you should try to help. However, each parent's concern must be, first and foremost, with the needs of his own child, and we have to recognize that an extremely difficult boy or girl needs the help of a specialist.

Most 9-to-12's like nothing better than to be with friends of their own age. But what about the loner? Should parents encourage him to join a group? Can they help him to make friends? A lot depends on the reasons why a child lacks companionship. It is not unusual for a child to go through a tem-

porary phase of preferring his own company, or that of adults—perhaps following some disappointment or upset—and he may simply need affectionate support from his parents to see him through a lonely patch. Some children seem perfectly content to spend much of their time alone, or with one or two close companions.

The true loner, however, may be deeply distressed by his inability to make friends. These are the children who, perhaps through fear, shyness, or feelings of inadequacy, find it especially hard to reach out to others. In extreme cases, if a child withdraws completely, or is frankly scared of mixing with other children, professional help may be needed. A different child, on the other hand, may simply need a little help in finding a suitable companion. The teacher may be able to suggest a child of similar interests whom parents could invite to their home. Outings, or small, simple parties may enable the shy child to overcome his anxiety, and begin building friendships.

In general, however, the parents of a solitary-seeming child can help best by bolstering their youngster's self-esteem, praising him for the things he is good at, and encouraging him to develop his particular interests. The shy child may then get a taste of society by joining a club that specializes in his chosen hobby: a bird-watching group, an orchestra, or a book club.

Frequently it is the solitary child who becomes the best student, and whose deep interests lead him to a career of distinction in later life. This may seem cold comfort to a parent who frets about him shut away in

While the majority of preteens tend to gather in groups, these will almost always be groups of the same sex. Loud scorn for the opposite sex is the order of the day, even though a 9-to-12-year-old may harbor a secret fondness for one of its members. Girls may moon over their love for a male pop star, teacher, or older boy, but more often than not, they are concerned with their latest crush on another girl or a woman teacher, while boys swear unflinching allegiance to their male pals, or hero worship some member of their own sex. Forgo any temptation to tease or cajole. This is your youngster's way of establishing his sexual role, of learning what it means to be a boy or a girl. Identification with others of the same sex is a necessary step on the road to sexual maturity.

If your child has a hobby he likes doing on his own, be glad that he can enjoy his own company. However, if you detect that his desire to be alone has roots in shyness and timidity with people, you might want to encourage him to join a group such as the Cadet Corps, or the Boy Scouts, so that he'll have the company of others of his own age.

his room reading a never-ending series of books on his favorite subject. However, it is important not to reveal this anxiety, or to fuss about his lack of friends. This will merely reinforce the child's own sense of inadequacy. The lonely child may need opportunities to talk over his feelings, but he should not be pressed to do so. What he needs above all is his parents' faith in him, and the reassurance that they love and respect him as he is.

At this age, too, the company of their own sex is a kind of protection from the anxiety a child may feel about the bodily changes he or she is beginning to undergo. As puberty approaches, a child is likely to become increasingly curious about sexual matters, and, although he may keep this curiosity from his parents, it will probably be a recurrent topic of discussion with his pals. The whispered speculations and dirty jokes that children share at this age are one way

of relieving apprehensions about a subject that is beginning to touch them so closely.

While your schoolage child may be reluctant to talk to you about sex, this doesn't mean that the subject should be a closed book between you. Although you may have answered his questions about sex, pregancy, and birth when he was much younger, he needs to be given this information again as he approaches puberty. It is sometimes surprising to parents just how often children need to be told the facts of life before they get them straight in their minds. As a child grows older, conflicting information from others, his own sometimes confused interpretations, and simple forgetfulness muddle the picture you presented earlier. Your previous frankness, however, and your willingness to go on answering his questions, or help him find out the facts, will encourage him to feel freer about asking you what he needs to know.

It is especially important to be alert to any particular anxieties that may lie behind a child's questions at this time. Whereas the young child was chiefly interested in knowing, the 9-to-12-year-old is beginning to relate these matters to himself, to his own sexual role, and his future development. "Doesn't it hurt terribly when a baby is born?" "But a baby is so big. How can it get out? Does it split the mother open?" "Is it painful when a man does that?" "What happens if the man wants to pass water?" "Can you get pregnant through kissing?" These are questions that commonly worry children at this, or a slightly later, stage. A straightforward and truthful explanation of the facts, with special reassurance on any points of anxiety, will help to dispel any fears and misconceptions picked up from other children.

What if your child doesn't ask any questions? There may be many reasons for this. Children generally feel shyer about this subject now, and may be embarrassed to ask about it, particularly if they sense a similar awkwardness on the part of their parents. Sometimes a child is confused about his feelings, or does not know how to ask what he wants to know. He may be getting enough information from other children— even if it is the wrong information—or have discovered it for himself in books. Whatever the reason, it is best not to force the issue by questioning him directly, or delivering a carefully prepared, formal explanation out of the blue. Often you can encourage a child to ask some question that will give you a lead. Questions may arise from conversations within the family, a TV program, or the arrival of a neighbor's baby, for instance. Even if your child does not show his curiosity openly, he may well give you indirect clues about the questions he would like to ask.

Questions about sex may give you an ideal

On the verge of their teens, young boys and girls begin to have a greater interest in the opposite sex, and a deeper interest in their own sexuality. The degree of interest varies from child to child.

chance to explain to your daughter about menstruation. Since girls today are maturing earlier, most doctors advise giving this information about the age of nine or so, or even earlier if a girl appears ready for it. Certainly by the time your daughter is becoming aware of physical changes in herself, you should prepare her for menstruation, if you have not already done so. You will need to explain simply but accurately how and why periods happen, pointing out that they are a natural, healthy part of womanhood.

Some women find it especially difficult to talk to their daughters about menstruation. We may see this development as a reminder that our once little girl is leaving childhood behind, and that we ourselves are growng older. We may recall our own adolescence, and find it hard not to pass on some of our

mixed feelings about what it means to be a woman. If we can come to terms with these feelings, our positive attitude toward our daughter's growth can help her as much as our factual explanations. It will help your daughter, too, if you show what to use for menstruation, telling her exactly how it is used, and letting her keep a stock of her own for when she needs it. Try to give her as much information about periods as you can, but be on the alert for any special fears or mistaken ideas she may have.

It is wise to explain menstruation within the whole context of sex and reproduction. Besides telling your daughter about the changes that are taking place in her body, it is important to discuss openly any feelings she may have about her physical development, or about her growing interest in boys,

Left: rough sports attract preteen and teenage boys strongly. A game such as football makes them feel they are proving themselves.

Right: a girl of the same age is often less physically active. It could be because she sooner becomes aware of puberty than boys.

and to tell her about the functioning of a boy's body, too.

Just as a girl will be interested in what happens to boys at puberty, so your son needs to know about menstruation, as well as being given information about his own development. Although puberty generally comes later for boys than for girls, a boy may start to mature physically at any time from the age of 10 or 11 onward. He, too, needs to be prepared for the bodily and emotional changes he can expect. It is important to explain to him, in advance, that he will have seminal emissions (wet dreams), and that these are a perfectly natural result of the accumulation of sperm and seminal fluid in his body. Again, this needs to be related to the whole story of sex and reproduction, with reassurance on any

particular points of apprehension (boys have just as many misconceptions and anxieties as girls). As with your daughter, your son should be told the facts about his developing interest in sex, and also about the growth and feelings of girls.

As the physical and emotional changes that mark the entry to adolescence begin, many preteens start to show obvious signs of tension. They may develop irritating tics, a habit of clearing their throat, twitching their nose, or biting their nails. They may feel guilty about their awakening sexual feelings, or ashamed of attempts to cope with them through masturbation. They may sometimes seem withdrawn or a little hostile toward their parents. Unless a child is showing excessive signs of stress, this is something to be lived with, not worried about. It is important for us to respect our youngster's growing need for privacy.

The best help we can give our child at this stage in his growth toward manhood or womanhood is through our own positive attitudes and teachings about sexuality. It is important to remember that guiding a child toward a healthy, satisfying life as a man or a woman goes far beyond giving him adequate information about sex. It is also a matter of how we ourselves view our sexual role, of how we react toward our children as boys or girls, and of how far we treat them as persons first, male or female second. As parents, we are the models on which a child will base his deepest feelings about his his own and the opposite sex. A child whose parents obviously enjoy their role as husband or wife, who respect each other, and value the equally important part that each has to play in their marriage, in the family, and in the life of the community, will gain a positive image of manhood or womanhood.

Of course, other people will now be influencing your child to some extent, too. As your youngster mixes with others outside the home, he is bound to encounter ideas, attitudes, and ways of doing things that differ from yours. How do you react when your child says: "Bart's mother lets him stay up till 11 o'clock. Why can't I?" "You know that word you told me not to say? Well, Nora's mother says it." "Why don't we get a big new car like Bobby's folks? Are we too poor?" "Why don't you go to church on Sundays?"

Feeling threatened, we may immediately leap into the attack: "I don't care what Bart's mother does. You'll do as I say!" "Nora's mother should know better!" "We all know how Bobby's folks love to swank." However, a child will inevitably go on making comparisons, and we can help him most by being willing to acknowledge and discuss the differences that do exist between people. We can explain why we hold certain beliefs, why we have chosen to live a particular way, or why certain standards are important to us. But we need to be objective, too. We want

94

The ten-year-old is boundlessly exuberant, but usually has the good sense to stop before getting overtired. A sense of responsibility is developing, so that a child of this age may often be trusted with caring for a pet. As for company, those of the same sex are preferred by far.

to avoid giving our child the impression of a black-and-white world where our beliefs are the only right ones, and others are all wrong. By talking out different attitudes and ideas openly and tolerantly, we not only help a child to discover the richness and variety of life, but we encourage him to begin thinking for himself.

There may, of course, be times when you feel you have to hold firm and tell your child: "I'm sorry, but I can't let you do what 'everybody else does.' You belong to our family, and we believe that this way is best for us." Or, "I know some people use those words, and maybe you enjoy saying them with other kids. But I don't like to hear them. In our home, they are not allowed." The important thing is to have considered your decision carefully, and to explain to your child why you have reached it.

This means that we, as parents, need to think through the standards that we consider essential for ourselves and our children, and those on which we may be prepared to give a little. On everyday questions, such as clothes, bedtimes, or a proposed jaunt with a friend, for example, we may feel that we can allow our child greater leeway. If we are ready to discuss the issue, we can often arrive at a sensible compromise. Johnny might be made to feel ridiculous if we insist he dress differently from the other kids. So, we can pick out half-a-dozen T-shirts of the right price that we can both live with, and let him select the two he likes best. He wants to go to bed later, but we feel that 11 o'clock is much too late. How about having him go to bed at the same time, but letting him read for half-an-hour? Or sticking to his usual

bedtime on school nights, but staying up an hour later on weekends? Yes, he can spend the whole day at the airport spotting planes with his pal, but only on condition that Dad picks both boys up on his way home from work. Provided we are willing to listen to a child's own viewpoint, and genuinely take it into consideration, he will be much more likely to accept our guidance on those occasions when we have to take a firm stand.

As children grow older, they need the opportunity to make more decisions for themselves, and we should give them the chance, wherever possible, to share in our thinking about the best way to act in a given situation, or how to solve some conflict within the family. There is no better way to do this than by open discussion in which each individual can put his views, and air his grievances.

Martha complains that Pete always plays his guitar at top volume when she is trying

When there's a family game time, or other way of spending time together, children will be less inclined to seek all their entertainment out of the home—or pursue friendships you don't approve of.

Who will do what and when? Is it fair for Mother to plan her chores as she wishes, but to insist that Sally always make her bed by a set time? Mom and Dad consider a certain TV program unsuitable viewing for Chuck. He thinks this is unjust. "You're always telling me to go off and watch TV when you're busy," he complains. "So why can't I see what I want?" Can the family plan some other activity for the time when the program is on? Could his parents arrange to watch TV with Chuck sometimes, and discuss the programs with him afterward? Jean doesn't see why she should let her parents know where she is going. "You never tell me when you'll be home," she protests. Maybe her parents can get into the habit of letting their children know where they will be, and when they will be back, calling up to explain delays, or leaving a note to welcome the children home when they can't be there.

By listening to our children we may find ourselves having to take a new look at some of our own reasons and attitudes. We may also find that, once encouraged, our children are remarkably ready to come up with workable solutions of their own. When children are allowed to share in family decision making, they are far more likely to stick to rules that they have suggested or helped to make. By respecting their needs and feelings, we can encourage them to give the same consideration to our needs and feelings. But family discussions don't have to center only on solving conflicts and making policy. There is fun to be had in sharing family activities, in laughing together, in telling each other jokes, and in sharing the funny experiences of our everyday lives. It is by this kind of open discussion and sharing—of family good times as well as bad—that we lay the groundwork for more effective communication during the stormier teenage years to come.

to do her homework. Can either child suggest a solution to the problem? Can Pete turn the volume down for a while? Is there a quieter room where Martha could do her homework? Can she do her homework earlier? Could Dad spend some time quietly with Pete while Martha works, or could Pete play his guitar at some other time? Mother needs more help in the house, so that she can have some time to herself. Which are the chores that we can share?

Talking with Your Teenager

6

"What's gotten into that child?" "Nothing I say makes the slightest impression on our 15-year-old." "Our teenager hardly says a word to us." "I daren't ask Nick where he's going or what he's doing; he just says it's none of my business." "I can't talk to that boy." "We just can't seem to communicate."

These are the kinds of comments thousands of bewildered parents are making about their teenagers. Their children often feel the same, too. "It's no use talking to my parents. They never listen." "I never tell my parents anything. They wouldn't understand." "They don't seem to care how I feel." "Talk to my parents—are you crazy? They hassle me enough as it is." "Everything I say sets off a row—so what's the use?" "People of their generation don't understand kids my age. We live in different worlds."

What has happened? Surely now that our child is growing up, verbal communication should be getting easier, not harder. Must all the good work we did in establishing open lines of communication with our children in earlier years come to nothing during adolescence? Is our sunny, outgoing child of a few years back bound to become a moody, uncommunicative teenager? How much rebellion is normal and necessary during adolescence? How much influence can we have over our teenagers? And how can we influence them at all if, as we fear, they won't even listen to us?

The thing to remember about those difficult teenage years is that they are most difficult for your teenager who is going through them. This is when your sympathy and understanding are most needed. If you have had good communications in the past, there should be no major breakdown at this time.

Life with a teenager can be pretty rough on a parent's ego, and it is not surprising if we sometimes find ourselves wishing that our child could leap from 12 to 20 without having to plow through the difficult years between. Probably your teenager wishes it, too. For parents who tell their youngster that the teens are the most wonderful and enjoyable years of his life have almost certainly forgotten the many moments of misery that adolescence can bring. This is a time when a teenager has to grapple with a host of physical and emotional changes that make him a puzzle even to himself. It is when we fail to understand the stresses and tensions he faces, and focus our attention on behavior rather than the reasons behind it, that the greatest conflicts can arise.

No longer a child, not yet an adult, a teenager is eager for independence, but desperately unsure of his ability to handle it. Back and forth he seesaws from childishness to maturity. Up and down swings his moods from elation to despair. Changes in body chemistry, more specific sexual feelings, psychological and social pressures, throw his emotions into turmoil. Unresolved conflicts from earlier years may reemerge now to demand fresh solutions. Academic and career pressures, the pace and shifting values of present-day society, add to the problems a teenager faces in his search for a sense of identity, and a basic philosophy by which he can live. Apparent apathy and indifference may cloak anxious self-questioning as the teenager asks: "Who am I?" "Where am I going?" "Why am I here?" Wild irritation, bursts of anger, sudden tears, or fits of giggling may stem from feelings of insecurity and

He's moody and bad-tempered at the moment. Maybe he even shouted hurtful things at you. It's not easy to be cool and calm about it, but try to remember that he may not even be able to explain his behavior to himself. He may be feeling as misunderstood and bewildered as you may be feeling hurt.

tensions that are hard for them to control.

Insecure he may feel, but a teenager has to work toward final independence from his parents if he is to become a responsible adult in his own right. Consequently, he may challenge our authority, resent it, and argue with us. He may become withdrawn and secretive, taking the telephone well out of earshot as he shares lengthy whispered confidences with a friend. A teenager cannot simply take over our standards without thinking them through for himself. Questioning our ideas and values is one way of establishing his own—even if they do turn out to resemble ours in the long run. Most teenagers need to see their parents in an unflattering light before they can come to terms with them as normal, fallible human beings. By criticizing our behavior, and calling attention to our faults, they make it easier to snip away at the strings of dependency.

Of course, this is painful for us. We, too, have mixed emotions as our children mature into young adults, and begin to grow away from us. When our teenager hits on our weak points, it hurts! Hard though it may be, however, this is a time when we need to choke back that bitter retort. When we allow ourselves to be drawn into counter-attack, real issues get lost in a welter of resentment and wounded feelings. It may be little comfort at times to tell ourselves that our teenager's behavior is par for the course, that "this too will pass." But it can help to remember that our teenager is far more bewildered by his feelings than we are. He can't explain to himself why he behaves as he does. If he could bring himself to say so, he would probably tell us that he dislikes some of his reactions as much as we do. As it is, his shifting moods may lead him to doubt what he really is like. Is he the concerned idealistic guy who last week gave his entire allowance to the poverty fund? Or the selfish, bad tempered grouch who bullied his kid sister, and yelled at his mother? Is she the confident, sunny angel who went to bed singing last night? Or the irritable, self-conscious creature who can hardly drag herself up in the morning? To

make matters worse a teenager has that terrible feeling that he will go on being miserable for ever.

No, it isn't always fun to be a teenager. While it may tax our patience to the limit, this is a time when we need to support and comfort our youngster, to be as compassionate and uncritical as we can. A teenager can feel pretty lonely and misunderstood at times. Bitter feuding with his parents only makes him feel lonelier still—convinced now that no one understands him—and he may

reject our guidance for this very reason.

How, then, can we help our teenager—and ourselves—to cope with this difficult phase, and come happily out of it? First of all, we need to remember that the teenage years are not all problems. Storms and turbulence there may be, but there will also be times of calmness and friendliness, of closeness and affection. In fact, many teenagers come through these years with skill and ease. The teens are not an isolated period in a youngster's life. They are simply

101

a special stage in the continuous process of his growth toward adulthood. How intensely a teenager rebels will depend on his past experience, on how much scope for independence he has already had, and on the kind of relationship that has grown up between child and parent over the years. Indeed, some experts in the field of parent-child communication maintain that rebellion and revolt need not be a part of adolescent development at all. If parents have kept the channels of communication open over the years, they say, there is no reason why the same constructive and healthy relationship should not continue during adolescence.

The key to meaningful communication between parent and teenager is mutual respect. We need to be willing to listen to our teenager, to examine his point of view, to show him that we respect his views and feelings. We need to let him know that, although we may not always agree with him, we respect his right to feel and think as he does. Perhaps our viewpoint *is* more reasonable. But when we tell our children, "You don't know what you're talking about," "We know better," "You're too young (too inexperienced, too dumb) to understand life as we do," we close the door on communication. A young teenager still needs the security that comes from group acceptance. The opinion of his peers means a great

The lines of communication are open, so mother and daughter are having a heart-to-heart chat that draws them closer as human beings. When the lines of communications are closed, father and son find that they can't talk out the problem.

deal to him. As he matures, he will need to start easing away from dependence on the group until he is able to stand confidently on his own feet. If he is to do this successfully, he needs to examine and evaluate his own ideas with the help of people he respects. We can be those people, provided we try to be honest with ourselves and with our children, and are prepared to treat them as persons in their own right.

Whereas communication now will be much easier if we have established an atmosphere of friendly respect and co-operation while a child was growing up, it is never too late to start. We can make up for past mistakes if we are willing to acknowledge them. We shouldn't be afraid to tell our children: "Looking back, I think I was a bit hard on you. I know I pooh-poohed your ideas sometimes, and I wish I hadn't. But I'm going to try to see that that doesn't happen any more." When we admit our mistakes, when we can say, "I'm sorry"— and mean it—our credibility with our children goes up. It is when parents strive always to appear in the right that they run the risk of losing their children's respect.

You may think they look a mess, and you may think that their rebelliousness is sham, but you can't deny that acceptance by their peers is one of the most important facts of life for them. You help your relationship with them most by accepting them as they are, and letting them know they are loved.

That doesn't mean that we should relinquish our role as parents. Far from it. Being a teenager, as one doctor describes it, is "like being offered a large and powerful motorbike, boasting of one's ability to handle it, but secretly hoping very much that somebody will help you control it. Or save you from having to put your apparent confidence in yourself to the test." Your teenager needs your help with the controls—though he would never admit it—and he will appreciate your support in establishing firm and worthwhile guides that he can follow. Those guidelines can be open to discussion and adjustment, but the important thing is that they exist. It is when parents sidestep their responsibility in these areas that their child gets the feeling, "Well, they don't care about me. They don't care what I do—so why not do whatever I feel like doing?" Guidelines can make you seem stern, but they prove you care.

Teenagers have a continuing need for the security of knowing that they are wanted, loved, and accepted by their parents. They need to know that we appreciate their feelings, and view their problems with compassion. But here we need to tread carefully. Listening sympathetically when your youngster wants to confide in you is one thing—constant probing of his feelings is quite another. Privacy is important to a teenager. He doesn't want to feel that his parents can see through him, that they understand everything about him. Nor is he comforted when we say, "I know, honey. I felt the same at your age." To him, his emotions are unique, mysterious, personal. Far better, then, to demonstrate that we accept those feelings than to analyze, judge, or belittle them. A heartfelt, "That's tough!" or "Looks like this is a rough time for you. I'd like to help if I can. I'm here if you need me," is

helpful. A sarcastic, "What happened? Was the world revolution called off?" or a would-be cheering, "All kids your age feel that way," "You'll feel better tomorrow," is not. To know when our youngster needs our understanding, and when he would rather work things out for himself, may require some delicate parental footwork.

Let's now look at some potential trouble spots between parents and teenagers, and see how we can use effective communication to handle them.

Take your teenager's hair and clothes, for example. "Leave me alone, can't you!" yelled Todd when his father tackled him for the umpteenth time about getting a haircut. "I've told you—it's my hair and I'll wear it the way I want it!" "But it's disgusting," persisted his father. "It's not even clean. I never thought a son of mine would end up trying to look like a sissy." "Who's a sissy? If you think you look so great, you should try looking in the mirror sometime," retorted Todd. With that, he stomped up to his room, and turned the record player on full blast.

Hairstyles and clothes have an important symbolic value for a teenager. They are a way of declaring his independence, of saying, "I am my own person. This is the way I want to be." Of course, he doesn't want to look like his parents. He wants to find a personality of his own. The way he dresses, the way he wears his hair, express his need to belong to his own age group, to demonstrate that he is a member of "us" and not of "them." It is essential to recognize just how important this need is to our teenager and, if possible, to refrain from joining battle over it. What happens when we do? Like Todd, your teenager will probably declare, "It's my hair," or, "I like these clothes. Why shouldn't I wear them?" "Do I tell you how to wear your hair?"

It doesn't help to poke fun at your teenager's appearance, or to tell him that he looks like a slob or a refugee from a circus. No one likes having their appearance criticized, and a teenager resents ridicule as

The teenagers' penchant for nonstop telephone talk can be a storm center in any home. For the sake of family peace, compromises may have to be made. One way to handle it may be to have the teenager pay part of the phone bill out of his or her earnings. Another solution may be to insist that the phone be left free for about half-an-hour between calls.

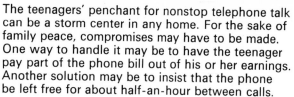

much as anyone else. If your teenager's tattered jeans, shapeless skirts, multi-colored beads, or tangled locks infuriate you, try asking yourself what it really is about these fashions that you find so hard to accept. A teenager will naturally resist any attempt to change his mode of dress, unless he can be convinced that it interferes in some concrete way with his parents' needs. You might ask that hair and clothes be clean, for example. "I'm sorry, son, but dirty hair at the dinner table spoils my appetite" is a legitimate expression of father's feelings. "I can't stand your hair that way," or "Those clothes are ugly and they don't suit you," attack a teenager's taste, and give no valid reason for change. Better to save your energy for more fundamental issues.

That's all very well, you might say, but how about when I'm expected to spend

hard-earned money on outlandish clothes? Many parents have found that the best way to handle this problem is to suggest that their teenager buy his own clothes out of his allowance, or money he has earned for himself. Most youngsters will ask for a higher allowance as they enter their teens. They need more money not just for clothes, bangles and beads, or cosmetics, but also for buying sports equipment, records, posters, and other items that are important to them. The happiest arrangement may be for parent and teenager to get together and negotiate a mutually acceptable allowance. Can you arrive at some compromise between the sum he would like, and the amount you can afford? Don't be swayed by arguments about the going rate for your neighborhood if this doesn't fit your budget. Rather than trying to convince your teenager that he doesn't need more money, you could tell

specific chores around the home, or reward him for any extra help he gives. Others have found that their children readily understand the need for family members to share various responsibilities in the home, and actually prefer that these tasks be unrelated to their allowances. "We feel," says one mother, "that our daughter's allowance is her share of family funds, a way of saying 'we're glad to have you around', not some kind of wages that have to be earned. I don't think you can teach kids about how people should help one another if they just do it because they're afraid their allowance will be cut off." Here is a question that each family must decide for itself, and one that lends itself to democratic discussion within the family. When we invite our youngster's participation in working out a solution to sharing chores, rather than imposing rules from above, we encourage cooperation as well as communication.

Talking over family policy can work equally well when it comes to other house rules—the use of the car and telephone, for example. One family tackled the car problem by agreeing that if their teenager used the car, he was to be responsible for keeping it clean, checking the oil and tires, and putting in his own gas. To save endless arguments over who should use the car when, they established a message center where Dad and teenage son gave each other advance notice about when they would need the car. "That message center was a godsend in other ways too," reports the mother of this family. "With everyone coming and going at different times, it was the ideal way of letting each other know: 'Won't be in to dinner tonight,' 'back at 10' or 'we have guests tomorrow at 7'." A family faced with an astronomical telephone bill agreed with their daughter that she should set aside some of her earnings from baby sitting toward her phone calls. In another family, mother agreed to make most of her calls during the day so long as her teenager left the phone free for about half-an-hour between calls in the evening. These were compromises

him truthfully, "We would like to give you more if we could, but our budget just won't stretch to it right now." Once you've given your youngster his allowance, however, it should be his to spend as he thinks fit. As one 15-year-old complains, "I saved up most of my allowance for weeks—and that meant going without movies and ball games, too—to buy a set of posters I wanted. My father was furious. He said I was wasting his money. Why bother to give me an allowance if he still considers it his money?"

When an allowance just isn't enough, young teenagers can usually find a way of supplementing it by taking on odd jobs in their neighborhood—baby sitting, mowing lawns, or washing cars, for example. Later, vacation jobs can give them wider opportunities for discovering what it is like to earn and handle money of their own. Some parents link their youngster's allowance to

brought about by frank discussion, and an honest sharing of family problems.

There are times, however, when you may need to support your teenager with a firm "no" over outings or activities that you consider unsuitable. Of course, your teenager will be enraged when you insist he leave that all-night party at 11:30, or won't let him have the car for a late double date. Remember how hard it is to take a stand against your peers when you're only 16. Your teenager would be the last to admit that he welcomes a way out of situations he isn't ready to handle, but you provide him with the face-saver he needs when he can say to his pals, "My parents sure are a drag with all their rules, aren't they?"

Whatever our family agreements over allowances or extra payments for chores, many of us consider that there is one occasion when we should reward our teenagers. A dollar or two for every A, or a gift for good test results is an incentive many parents hold out in hopes of encouraging greater effort at school. The trouble is that this idea can also misfire. Not only do we fail to encourage a youngster to enjoy learning for its own sake, but when we attach material rewards to high marks we may undermine his self-esteem. Few children

want to do badly in school, but intellectual abilities vary. A few gifted youngsters may achieve high grades with a minimum of work; others only at the cost of tremendous effort; still others may obtain only average grades no matter how hard they try.

If our youngster is failing, let's try to find out why. Are we expecting too much? Is there some physical or emotional problem that is holding him up? If he is doing well, of course we are pleased. But don't let's give him the impression that our approval depends on his success. Better to say, "Those are good grades. You must be glad you worked so hard," than to tell him, "We're proud of you. You've earned your reward." If we want to give him a reward, how about giving it before his test results—for the effort—rather than after, as if linked only to his success.

"I hate school," declared Janice, "it's so boring." "The things they teach us— they're worthless, irrelevant," rages Elliott. "That stupid woman—she dishes out twice as much work as the other teachers. I hate her!" storms Helen. Remarks like these can send a parent's anxiety level soaring. "Now, dear, you know you need a good education if you're to get the kind of job you want," we preach, or "Well, the teacher must know

Gym may be fun to some, and studying Shakespeare may be to others, but along with the fun in high school go many pressures. High schoolers are not only worrying about what they want to do in life, but also have fears that college entry will be impossible if they don't meet the heavy competition.

109

Young love is the stuff poetry and songs are made of—but mother and father worry deeply over their teenagers' attitude toward sexual behavior. It helps to know that in spite of their seeming sophistication, teenagers are seeking guidelines.

what she's doing. Perhaps you should try a little harder." Well-meaning though they may be, these reactions act as communication stoppers. They tell our youngster, "Your feelings don't matter."

We needn't agree with our teenager's judgment of school or of his teacher, but we can accept his current feelings about them. A willingness to listen to his grumbles will help him to release his feelings, and define his real concerns more clearly. Maybe he has simply had a couple of monotonous lessons that day. Perhaps he is feeling the pressure of forthcoming tests. Maybe his ideas were criticized in class. Is he wondering what kind of job he wants to do later on? Does he resent the physics teacher because physics is a subject he finds hard, and he is afraid of slipping behind? We will only find out if we listen. Then we can offer advice.

Listening with understanding helps, too, during your youngster's first tentative relationships with the opposite sex. A lovelorn teenager doesn't want to be told, "There are plenty more fish in the sea," or "You'll get over it," any more than we would in similar circumstances. We have only to think back to our own adolescent anxieties to sympathize with the teenager who worries, "I'll never get a boyfriend," or "I don't know what to say to girls." If going steady is the "in" thing, it probably won't help to tell your daughter she should "play the field." Remember, steadies have a habit of changing of their own accord over the months. Sometimes a steady is merely an insurance against too many dateless weekends, and then it may help to point out the advantages of getting to know other people, too. But by the time they reach mid-adolescence, many of today's teenagers regard dating a succession of different people weekly as un-

acceptable behavior. Wise parents encourage their teenager to bring his or her friend into their home, as well as remaining firm about homecoming times, knowing where their teenager can be reached if necessary, and having him call to save them too much worry if he is delayed.

It is difficult to see our teenager dating a boy or girl we consider unsuitable, but most parents have found it inadvisable to criticize. Friendships we disapprove of tend to end more quickly if we don't resist them too vigorously. If, instead, we welcome our teenager's friends into our home, not only will we get to know them better, but also he, too, will have a chance to see them against the background in which he has been raised. There are parents, on the other hand, who are more concerned about their youngster's apparent lack of popularity, and who push him into dating before he is ready for it. This is not a good idea. Such pressures can add to a teenager's feelings of insecurity. If your son or daughter still prefers baseball to dancing, or reading to parties, leave well enough alone. It won't be long before you wonder what you were worried about.

The issue that does go on worrying parents, of course, is their teenager's attitude toward sexual behavior. What you tell your teenager about moral standards will, of course, depend on your own convictions. Each of us has our opinions of what is right and what is wrong in sexual matters, but we seldom take the time to think through our beliefs. If we want to communicate our values to our teenagers, we need to tell them not only what our views are, but also why we hold those views. These topics should not be presented as lectures, but they can be introduced into ordinary discussions that take place in the presence of your teenager.

Let him join in the conversation, or argue against you if he wishes, without belittling or discounting his point of view. Often, teenagers shock their parents by saying, "What's wrong with it if we love each other?" "A lot of the girls I know sleep with their boyfriends. Why shouldn't they?" "We all

A family that does things together is most often a family in which parents and children can talk to each other at any age. It always helps if parents take a genuine interest in the subjects and activities their children find exciting and rewarding.

know it's fairly safe nowadays—so why not?" Before we react with alarm, we need to remember one important point: teenagers are rarely as sophisticated or self-confident as they would like to appear, and their remarks do not necessarily represent their own point of view. They are perplexed, and they want realistic guidelines.

Teenagers are looking for a system of values and standards that they can live by. They are distressed by the hypocrisy of a society which preaches one set of values, yet so patently practices another. It is up to us to know clearly what we stand for and why, and to demonstrate that we try to uphold our beliefs in our own lives. It is when we can be convincing models, and when we are prepared for open discussion with our teenager not just about sex, but also about love, commitment and respect for the feelings of others, that we help him to sort out his own thinking, and formulate a positive philosophy on handling sex wisely. Nor should we forget the influence of self-esteem on sexual behavior. When your youngster's self-esteem is high, he will be far better equipped to take his own firm stand on moral issues.

The same attitude holds true when it comes to another anxious aspect of the teenage years: drug taking. Mutual discussions on this topic will impress your teenager far more than dire threats and warnings. While it is essential that we explain the frightening dangers of drugs to our teenager, we need to ensure that what we say is based on fact. If we make inaccurate statements, our youngster is not likely to place much faith in our guidance on the subject. The wisest policy is to listen carefully to your teenager's own information—and misinformation—to discuss his arguments calmly, and to make it clear that your views are firm and reasonable ones, drawn from knowledge, not prejudice. We must also bear in mind, of course, that if we ourselves drink, or smoke cigarettes, we will have a much harder time justifying some of our arguments against these and other drugs. Suggestions for tackling this issue, and answering some of the other tricky questions that teenagers may raise about both drugs and sex, appear in the Questions & Answers section of this book.

Sometimes we have to face the fact that

we are the last people in whom our teen-agers want to confide. Although we may feel hurt when our son or daughter prefers to share some private affair with friends, or even other adults outside the family, we should not interpret this as a lack of trust, or a breakdown in communication. There are simply times when it is easier for a teenager to work through his feelings with people to whom he is less emotionally attached.

We will, on the other hand, find it a great deal easier to keep in touch with our teenagers if we are ready to take a genuine interest in the subjects that excite and interest them. School, pop music, science fiction, oriental religions, ecology, politics, ethics, revolution, poverty—these are topics on which you can find your teenager eager to express his opinion when he knows you want to hear it. We help our teenagers—and ourselves—when we are alive to modern problems, open to new ideas and new ways of thinking, and truly concerned with the people and the world around us.

Parents or Pals?
7

Family life consists of a long series of readjustments. Parents as well as children grow and change over the years, and both must adapt to changes within themselves, and in their relationship with each other. This is never more apparent, or perhaps more difficult, than during the teenage years when our children grow away from us, and we must be prepared to let them go.

As our teenagers become young adults, we, too, may be faced with a sometimes painful reassessment of our own lives. Do we see in our teenagers an unwelcome reminder that we are no longer young? Do they make us recall with regret the things we had hoped to do with our lives? Are we pressuring them to realize our own unfulfilled ambitions? Are we perhaps resentful of their seemingly greater opportunities, or envious of their youthful good looks and vitality? Of course, we have made a tremendous emotional investment in our children all through their growing years, but has that investment been so great that we have not found time for our marriage, for other interests, for ourselves? Are we rushing to make a last desperate attempt to influence our teenager before it is too late? Do we feel depressed at the increasing loss of our parental authority, and wonder how we can forge new links with our now grownup child on an adult-to-adult basis?

Few of us escape at least some mixed emotions as we see our teenagers standing on the threshold of adulthood. The very fact of acknowledging such feelings can help us to come to terms with them. It is when resentments are left to simmer, unrecognized beneath the surface, that they are most likely to play their part in provoking parent–teenager conflict. An explosion of rage at his son's tight jeans, or his daughter's refusal to wear a bra, for example, may sometimes stem from father's anxiety over his own waning youth and vigor. An indignant attack on "the morals of the younger generation" may cloak dissatisfaction with the apparently humdrum routine of his own life. "I'm ashamed to admit it," confesses one mother, "but I feel jealous of my daughter. There am I trying desperately to lose weight, smooth over wrinkles, and cover up gray hairs, while she goes around without a bit of make-up, in the most outrageous clothes—and still looks beautiful."

It isn't easy to admit that we may actually be envious of our own sons or daughters, but this is a perfectly natural and human reaction—as we will find out if we share our feelings with other parents. "It was only when I began to talk things over with my husband and one or two close friends," says the mother already mentioned, "that I realized I wasn't being a selfish or bad mother because I feel this way. I still love my daughter just as much. In fact, talking about my feelings made me realize that I'm also proud that she has grown into such a lively, pretty girl. Think how disappointed I might have been if she'd turned out dull and unattractive."

He's sullen and withdrawn after you've had angry words, and now you're wondering how deep the hurt is. Such tempests can be frequent during your child's teenage years, and it takes understanding and effort to heal the breach—but it can be done.

As parents, we want the best for our children, but we aren't monsters if, while offering them chances that we never had, we still feel an occasional pang of regret at our own missed opportunities. It is when parents fail to acknowledge the way they feel that they may overload their children with an unnecessary burden of guilt. Jeff's mother, for example, had always regretted not going to college, and was determined that her son should. He did, but only months after entering college, he announced his intention of dropping out. "I just can't stand it," he explained. "Mother is always getting on my back, wanting to know exactly what I'm doing in school, that kind of thing. She doesn't say so, but I know she's thinking, 'if only I had your chances'. It makes me feel that I don't deserve to go to college, or

Your teenagers lead a busy life in high school, often taking up extra-curricular activities, such as band, besides classroom work, such as language laboratory. It's up to you to encourage them without adding an-other degree of pressure.

that I'm only doing it for her, not for myself."

It is a temptation to try to relive our youth through our teenagers, so we need to stand back and ask ourselves, "Whose life is it?" It is unfair to make our teenagers the vehicle for our own frustrated ambitions. We all know examples of parents who try to push their children into fields they themselves would have liked to have chosen, or that they never managed to enter: the failed singer or actress who wants her youngster to become a star; the would-be scientist or doctor who opposes his son or daughter's desire for a journalistic career. As our teenager approaches the difficult decision about what to do with his future, we need to examine his or her potential and talents carefully and realistically. If your son or daughter is not college material, don't worry. He or she may be much happier and more successful in another, less academic field. Nagging or overambitious parents can be a torment to an adolescent who feels that he must try to please them. This is an unfair, added pressure to a teenager's already overpressured life.

Adolescents in their mid- to late teens are in a most difficult position. At a time when they may still feel uncertain about their lives, and very unsure of themselves, they are called upon to make fundamental decisions and plans for the future. It is at this stage that they must try to pass examinations in order to achieve high school diplomas, work for high grades if they wish to go to college, contemplate the taking of scholastic aptitude tests. They must choose whether or not to go on to some form of higher education in the liberal arts, or take more specialized training. Boys and girls have to think of directing their energies toward a specific career that they will want to pursue.

Sometimes the pressures on these grownup children seem almost unbearable. "We're not the ones who are pushing our son," says one mother. "It's he who is driving himself to the point of exhaustion. He is

117

You've probably heard your older teenager complain that "school is irrelevant". An experiment in Denver is trying to bring more relevance into school study. A lesson in teamwork comes in shooting rapids. Hard manual labor is learned by garbage collection. Work on an Indian reservation teaches human relations.

set on getting into one particular college, and we're terribly worried about what will happen if he is turned down." This is a problem familiar to many parents. For, quite apart from any feeling that his parents are anxious for him to do well, a teenager may set too high standards for himself. His school may lay great stress on the importance of going to college—or to a certain college— and pressures for high grades and college entrance come from peers, too. If we tell our teenager to "stop worrying," or "just do the best you can," he may feel that we

don't understand what he is going through. Better to let him know that we recognize the strain he is undergoing, and sympathize with his anxieties.

While acknowledging his feelings, however, we should emphasize that whether or not he gets into the college of his choice, or another college, or doesn't go to college at all, it is all right with us. Sheer numbers mean that many youngsters will not get into their first choice of college, no matter how intelligent they are, or how hard they try. In fact, as some child psychiatrists have pointed out, many students feel let down and disappointed when they finally do reach college, simply because they had such unrealistically high expectations of what they would find there as part of college life.

We can point out to our youngster that it is what he learns that matters, not where he learns it. Whether a teenager goes to college or not, the important thing is what he himself makes of his own life, how he develops his particular talents and interests, and the kind of human being he is. We don't stop learning when we leave school or college. In fact, as many a college graduate has remarked, a person's real education may only begin after university, when he faces the problem of finding his place in the world as a truly independent and responsible adult. Quiet encouragement, and the reassurance that we are happy with his accomplishments and will stand by him in his choice for the future, are the most positive ways of helping an unsure teenager who is facing a mounting series of increasingly demanding academic hurdles.

Only a few fortunate youngsters know from the outset what kind of trade or profession they want to follow. Most will change their minds several times before settling on a particular field. Talking with your teenager about the kind of work he would dislike—and why—as well as discussing the subjects that interest him, can help him to clarify his thoughts about the type of career he might eventually take up. We can also encourage our youngster to look into a wide range of vocational fields, to try his hand at a variety of vacation jobs, to talk to people already working in professions that might appeal to him, and to discuss job and educational options with a trained counselor. Sometimes the best gift we can give a pressured teenager is time. Taking a year off from school to work, for example, may give some youngsters the chance they need to discover where their true preferences lie. Just letting him know that he doesn't have to make a once-for-all decision right away can open the way for a more realistic choice later.

That doesn't mean that we should not offer our teenagers advice. We owe it to them to make our views known. We can say, for example, "O.K. So you want to be a pop musician. But that's a risky profession. You may need to find some other work between engagements. We feel it would be a good idea if you finished college first. You could still go on with your music part-time. Then if you need to find a job later, or you change your mind, you'll have the qualifications you need."

However, we may well have to face the fact that, when our youngster finally does make up his mind about a career, his choice may be entirely different from ours. Bob's father, for instance, had long cherished the idea that Bob would join him in his business. But Bob was determined to do social work. Cheryl's parents would have liked her to become a teacher, and were disappointed when she turned to dress designing. John's mother wanted him to be a lawyer, but her son decided to become an aircraft mechanic. Dora's mother had hoped for a glamorous career for her daughter. Dora's choice of being a librarian seemed dull by comparison.

Of course, we are going to feel some disappointment if our teenager's way is not our way. But it doesn't help to rage, "After all we've done for you! Throwing a good education down the drain! Is this all the thanks we get?" We may say we would have liked him to have chosen otherwise. We may admit we would like to persuade him

120

to change his mind. We can tell him why. But in the end we must be able to say, "Whatever your own final decision, we will back you up." Remember, a youngster who unwillingly falls in with his parents' wishes may go on harboring a deep resentment against them for not respecting his individual needs and abilities. When we can step back and let our older teenager live his own life, confident that he is doing what he feels is right for him, and working toward the fulfillment of his own potential, he can come back freely to meet us on a more mature level as a person in his own right.

It is also important to remember that our teenagers want us to act like concerned and responsible grownups. There can be few sadder—or, to a teenager, more embarrassing—spectacles than a parent pretending to be 17 again. Yet some of us, caught up in the current cult of youth, and desperately anxious to remain in touch with our teenagers, make frenzied attempts to copy their behavior, language, social activities, and dress. An older teenager will usually have outgrown the stage of openly criticizing his parents, and may well be too compassionate to tell them to "act their age." But he can suffer agonies of embarrassment over their behavior just the same. As one teenager put it, "You're a neat dresser, Mom, but thank goodness you look like a mother."

How, then, can you stay in touch with your older teenager? The main thing is to try to convey to this growing young adult that you respect his new status. After all, society today generally regards a young person as a fully fledged adult at the age of 18. If society acknowledges this, we cannot possibly continue to overprotect our teenager, and treat him like a child. Let him go now, but emphasize that you will always be there if he needs you. At this age, too, he will sometimes feel like crawling back into bed to enjoy a little extra pampering when the going gets rough. There are times when he or she may need you desperately: when a romance breaks down, when an exam is failed, when he has come down with a bout

Taking a trip on their own is one way teenagers can learn greater independence and self-reliance.

At what age is your son or daughter considered an adult under the law? When can your children do as they like about driving, working, going to school? Legal rights as adults vary from state to state, although everyone can now vote at the age of 18. This chart summarizes the age laws for some activities that a person under a given age cannot legally do. Until then, responsibility lies with the natural guardian—usually the father—or a legal guardian. A mother is guardian if the father is dead, of if she has custody after a divorce.

◆ Anyone 18 years old and married is considered an adult.
■ A married woman is considered an adult.
△ At 16 with written parental consent.
* At 16 with notarized consent of a parent or guardian.
● At 16 after driver education course, if parent signs application.
▲ A provisional license at 18 (16 upon completion of driver education course).
†† A married person of any age is considered an adult.
☐ Valid only 5 a.m. to 8 p.m. unless accompanied by a parent or guardian.
** A woman married to a man over 21 is regarded as an adult.
† Or until graduation from high school if this occurs before the age of 18.
★ With driver education.

No Longer a Child!

State	Age of Majority	Driving License Provisional License (PL) Junior License (JL)	Work	Work with Work Permit	Ages of Compulsory Education
Alabama	21♦	16	17	16	7–16
Alaska	19■	18△	16	No Law	7–16
Arizona	21♦	18*	16	14	8–16
Arkansas	21M, 18F	18△	16	14	7–16
California	21	18●	18	15	8–18
Colorado	21	21, 18PL, 16JL	16	14	7–16
Connecticut	21	21▲	18	16	7–16
Delaware	21	18●	18	14	6–16
Florida	21††	18△	18	16	7–16
Georgia	21	16	18	16	7–16
Hawaii	20	20, 15 with parental consent	18	16	6–18
Idaho	21M, 18F	16, 14JL★	14	No Law	7–18
Illinois	21M, 18F	21 ; 18 with parental consent●	16	14	7–16
Indiana	21	18 ; 16½ with parental consent	18	14	7–16
Iowa	21††	16★, 14JL	16	14	7–16
Kansas	21	16, 14JL	16	14	7–16
Kentucky	18	18△	18	16	7–16
Louisiana	21♦	17, 15JL	18	16	7–16
Maine	20	18 ; 17 with parental consent	16	No Law	7–17
Maryland	21	21 ; 18 with parental consent●	18	16	7–16
Massachusetts	21	18, 17JL, 16½JL★	18	16	7–16
Michigan	21††	18●, 14JL	18	14	6–16
Minnesota	21	18●, 16JL	16	14	7–16
Mississippi	21	15	14	No Law	7–16
Missouri	21	16, 15JL★	16	14	7–16
Montana	21M, 18F††	18△, 15★	18	16	7–16
Nebraska	20††	16	16	14	7–16
Nevada	21M, 18F	18△	17	14	7–17
New Hampshire	21	18●	18	12	6–16
New Jersey	21	17 ; 16 agricultural license	18	16	6–16
New Mexico	21††	16, 15★	16	14	6–17
New York	21	18, 17★, 16JL□	18	16	6–16
North Carolina	21	18●	18	16	7–16
North Dakota	21M, 18F	16, 14JL	16	14	7–16
Ohio	21	18●	18	16	6–18
Oklahoma	21M, 18F	16, 15½★	16	14	7–18
Oregon	21††	16, 14JL	18	14	7–18
Pennsylvania	21	18	18	16	8–17
Rhode Island	21	18, 16★	18	16	7–16
South Carolina	21	16, 15JL	16	No Law	7–16
South Dakota	21M, 18F††	16, 14JL	16	14	7–16
Tennessee	21	16, 14JL	18	14	7–17
Texas	21††	18●, 15JL★	15	No Law	7–17
Utah	21M, 18F††	16★	18	14	6–18
Vermont	21††	18, 16JL	16	14	7–16
Virginia	21	18●	18	16	7–16
Washington	21**	18●	18	14M, 16F	8–16
West Virginia	21	18, 16JL	16	under 16	7–16
Wisconsin	21††	18●, 14JL	18	16	7–18†
Wyoming	21	21△	16	under 16	7–17
District of Colombia	21	18△	18	14	7–16

Will my child so rebel against convention that he or she becomes a dropout? This is a common fear of parents today. The idea that your son might go to India to loaf rather than to enjoy travel is not a happy one. It may be an unpleasant jolt if your child joins a commune, even if there is a formal wedding. Nor does the uninhibited dance of a girl at a pop festival appeal to you. If these things happen, conciliation may be hard, but not at all impossible.

of flu. While respecting his status as an adult, keep the door open for those times when he might feel like backtracking a bit.

The feeling that his parents and teachers trust him, and respect his new maturity and independence, encourage a teenager to see us differently, too. Overcritical attitudes are replaced by more realistic views. He may now feel like entertaining at home, and even welcome a brief appearance of his parents. He is beginning to see his parents as people, not just symbols of authority.

It will be an odd moment when your teenager reveals that he sees you as a person, "warts and all," and doesn't condemn you for any faults he can now discern. For a moment, you may feel like reacting in the old ways, out of sheer habit ("Look here, Janet—none of your sass." "Have some respect." "Remember, I am your mother.") But now, above all, is a time to drop those well-worn responses, to react with some humor—to admit it when your son or daughter has hit on a sore point. ("Yes, dear, you're right, I do have an atrocious temper. I hope it hasn't been too rough on you all these years. At least it's over quickly— but then so's an earthquake.") Chances are that the realization that you can be yourself will come as a great relief to both of you, and your teenager will respond with obvious pleasure and relief, too.

What happens, however, when there has been a break in your relationship with your teenager? How can you get back in touch after something has gone wrong? Eighteen-year-old Ellen, for example, went to live with a considerably older man of whom her parents fully disapproved. They threatened that, unless she broke off this relationship, they would "have nothing more to do with her." In due course, the affair ended of its own accord. Another girl, Belinda, became a fervent member of a new religious movement. She rejected her parents as not being "true Christians," and left home. Later, when the leader of the movement "lost his faith," Belinda, too, grew disillusioned, and returned to her family. Warren, 19, dropped out of college, and spent a year living in a commune, hitchhiking abroad, and experimenting with drugs before deciding (like more than 70 per cent of college dropouts) to go back and study for his bachelor's degree.

In situations like these, reconciliation between parent and teenager will not usually result from a single heart-to-heart talk. It will need understanding, goodwill, and perseverance on both sides. Above all, it will probably need time. Parents may wonder, "where did we go wrong?" Their teenager may feel a sense of guilt, despite his attempts to conceal it. Both may need to try to forget hurtful things that have been said, and each must avoid the temptation to voice a sweeping condemnation of the other's behavior. In some cases, professional counseling may help. But the majority of parents and teenagers can, with honesty and a genuine desire to rebuild their relationship, close the gap that has opened between them.

It is often said that a parent's whole task is to work himself out of a job. We must prepare our children for the time when they can stand on their own feet, independent of us. That is why it is important for us, too, to give some thought to our future, preferably even before our children enter adolescence. "I feel so lost," said one mother as she saw her youngest off to college. "What is there left for me now?" "Hey," replied her husband, "What about *us*, you mean. We were the ones who started this whole thing off—remember?"

At this stage in their lives, husband and wife may need to take a fresh look at them-

The joy of seeing your child on the threshold of adulthood is immeasurable—but it is not untinged with sadness as well. We can't help thinking that he will soon be leaving home, and we wonder if we will be able to keep our relationship close.

selves, and at their relationship. Have we kept up with each other's growth and changing needs over the years? Can we—do we—talk to each other honestly about our feelings, our differences, our plans for the future? Do we listen—really listen—to each other? Have we, in fact, tried to keep the lines of communication open between ourselves, as well as our children? If not, can we start trying now?

As our children grow up, we need to remember that we are persons as well as parents, and that we may have 20, 30 or 40 years of living ahead of us after they leave home. That isn't just time to be filled, but time for fulfillment. Just as our teenagers must find occupations suited to their particular aptitudes, so we can take stock of our talents, abilities, interests, and concerns, and plan ahead for a new and satisfying way of life. The more fully we can be ourselves and live our own lives, the easier we will find it to let our children live theirs, and the richer will be our relationship with them.

Of course, our children will always be our children, and will remain a central focus of our lives. But as parents, we have to ask ourselves, "What do we really want for our children?" We have to mean it when we say, "Most of all we want them to be happy—in their own way." Of course we've made mistakes. Who hasn't? Mistakes are part of life itself. But if we have tried to raise our children with understanding and affection, that is what counts. Now we must be able to stand back and admire our good work. Loving and letting go isn't easy, but if we can achieve this last task of parenthood, we can reap one of parenthood's greatest rewards. For, our children will want to return, and now, as adults, they can become our closest, dearest, and most loyal friends.

Questions & Answers

A child's questions call for honest answers. But what can you say to a child who asks, "When are you going to die, Mommy?" How can you reassure a preschooler who has to go to the hospital? When, and what, should you tell your toddler about a coming baby? How can you warn a child about sexually disturbed adults? What should parents tell their teenagers about sex, birth control, drugs, dating? How do you answer the argument that "everybody else is doing it," or, "you drink alcohol, so why shouldn't I smoke pot?" Can you make your standards of behavior sound reasonable to your teenager? What advice can you give him about premarital sex or about promiscuity? Are there ways to ease family friction when living with a moody teenager? How can you get your teenager to keep to his curfew, and get home on time?

These are some of the questions that all parents have to face sooner or later, and the kinds of problems on which they must try to offer their children practical help and guidance. No one can tell you exactly what to say to your child. That will depend on your personality and beliefs, and on your knowledge of your own particular child. However, suggestions about the kind of response we might use, or that other parents have found useful, can often help us to sort out our own thoughts, and present our ideas more easily.

Here, then, are some specific questions and answers arising out of themes discussed in this book, and dealing with topics of concern to all parents today. Some of the suggestions may not suit your thinking, or your child, but others may give you a frame of reference in which to formulate your own individual response to your child. For, whatever we say to our children, the most important thing is to listen to what they are asking—really listen, from the heart—and to demonstrate our willingness to see their problems from their point of view. That is how we create an atmosphere in which we can offer our children the greatest support and understanding. That is what makes the difference between talking *to* and talking *with* your child.

You feel so close, loving and tender toward your growing child, and you wonder how you can retain the feelings throughout life. One of the answers lies in creating and keeping full communication.

129

Some Childhood Fears

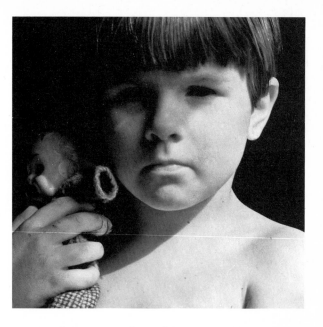

Gideon, now 7 months old, clings to me and cries every time his father comes near him. My husband is naturally upset by this, and so am I. What can be wrong?

Surprising though it may seem, this is a normal phase in your baby's development. Whereas a young baby may start out by responding happily to most of the people around him, by the age of seven or eight months he is likely to show some alarm in the presence of anybody, or anything, that seems unfamiliar. Doctors call this "stranger anxiety", and think it may be partly due to the baby's growing ability to distinguish between friend and stranger. Babies differ in their reactions at this stage. Some cling exclusively to just two people—their parents. Others want only their mother. This is naturally upsetting for fathers, who find themselves regarded as outsiders when they reappear at the end of the day, and who may become jealous of the exclusive attachment between mother and baby. That is why it is so important for both parents to be aware of what this phase means, and to realize that it will pass. The baby will get used to his father again, even though he may need longer to adjust to other people. "Stranger anxiety" is commonest between the ages of five and ten months, although it may not occur until a child is a year old. The best approach during this stage is to protect your baby from too many new faces and places, and to let visitors know that he needs a little time before making friends.

I have to go to the hospital for several days, leaving my three-year-old in the care of my mother. How can I prepare my daughter for this separation without alarming her?

The best way to help your child is to tell her in advance that you will be going to the hospital. Children can face up to a necessary separation far better if it has been carefully explained to them beforehand. Parents who slip away while their child is asleep, or staying with a relative, can cause him great distress. One of a child's deepest fears is of being abandoned by his parents, and if parents must leave him for any length of time, he needs constant reassurance that they still love him, and will return. So remember to tell your daughter when you hope to be back. Perhaps a week or so before your departure, you could explain that you are going to the hospital to get well, that you love her and will think of her all the time, and will miss her very much. Tell her, too, that you will be home by a certain day, and then you will both be very happy together again. Explain in as much detail as possible what will happen while you are gone: how Grandma will take care of her, the things they will do together, how she will play with Daddy in the evenings, how they will think of Mommy and miss her, and so on. Repeat these comforting reassurances several times, even if your child doesn't seem particularly interested at first, and try acting out the events you are describing with the aid of toys. It will help if your daughter can remain in the familiar surroundings of her own home while you are gone, and if Daddy and Grandma often talk to her about you, and about the time when the family will all be together again. Photos of you around the house, and talks on the telephone will all help to make even this short absence more bearable.

Supposing a child has to go to the hospital himself. What should he be told about this?

Tell him the truth above all. This is a time when your child must be able to trust you, and, if he has been deceived, it will be very hard to reassure him. What you tell your child will, of course, depend on his age, and the reason for his stay in hospital. In general, however, it is wise to give your child as much information as he can understand about why he is going to the hospital, and what to expect while he is there. If he is to have an operation, you can tell him the purpose of it without going into too many frightening details. But, remembering that some hospital procedures—blood tests or injections, for example—are likely to be unpleasant, it is best not to pretend that hospital will be fun, or that nothing nasty will happen. You could say, for instance, that sometimes the doctors and nurses do things we don't like, but they only do them to help us get well. It is especially important to explain to your child about anesthesia, and to stress that this is a "special kind of sleep" that will last only a short time, and will prevent him from feeling any pain during the operation. Warn him, however, that he will probably feel sore after the operation. Reassure him that the operation will not change or damage him in any way, but tell him in advance of any obvious after effects, like a scar or stitches. Such preparation is best begun a week or two in advance for a schoolage child, so that he will have time to discuss any fears or misconceptions. In the case of a younger child, it is wiser to wait until two or three days before he goes to the hospital. Here again, you can help your child by playing out the situation beforehand, using dolls to rehearse the coming events. Stories and picture books about hospitals can also help. Some parents even arrange to visit the hospital with their child beforehand. Many hospitals now allow parents to stay with children under five, and you should certainly arrange to do this if at all possible. Try to be with your child when he wakes up after surgery, and spend as much time with him as you can. Let him talk out his feelings about the hospital and what has happened to him. It is only natural for him to feel upset at so much discomfort; but so long as you have prepared him well, he should not suffer any long lasting effects.

How can I help my child to be less afraid of visits to the doctor?

The most important thing is to acknowledge that your child *is* afraid, and to let him know that you understand his feelings. Most of us try to reassure our children by telling them, "It won't hurt," "There is nothing to be scared of," or "There's no need to cry." This really isn't helpful. It doesn't take away the pain or the fear, and only makes the child feel more miserable and misunderstood. Far better to tell your child truthfully what is to happen. The day before the visit, let him know what the doctor is likely to do to him, the kind of instruments he will use, or the tests he may do. If there is to be an injection, tell him that it may hurt a bit, and that he may have to cry, but you will be there to hold his hand until it is over.

Have you any advice on getting children used to a baby sitter? My two start to scream as soon as we try to leave the house.

It is a good idea to have your sitter come as early as possible, especially if he or she is someone unfamiliar to your children. In this way, your children will have time to become accustomed to their sitter while you are still around. The children will take their cues from you, and if they see you getting along well with this apparently friendly new person, the chances are that they will too. You will also have time to explain your children's habits and needs to the sitter. It may seem costly to have to pay for extra hours of baby sitting, but it can be worth it in emotional terms. All too often, parents get all ready, and depart as soon as the baby sitter arrives, leaving her to cope with an upset or anxious child. Worse still, they may wait until the children are asleep, and then slip away. This can be disturbing for a young child. Imagine yourself waking up to find a complete stranger staring at you in the dark. One experience like this can be enough to make a child frightened of going to sleep, and will certainly cause him to be more upset next time you go out. In general, it is best to have sitters your children know—neighbors, friends, or relatives—or to continue with the same one or two sitters once they have built up a good relationship with your children. It may also help if you tell your children in advance that you will be going out, and who will be coming to look after them, and talk to them about the things they will do while you are gone. If your children complain bitterly about a sitter, or if it appears that something about her has upset or frightened them, it would be wise not to engage the same person again, or perhaps even to consider whether you may be leaving them too often. Once prepared for the experience, however, and if left with a friendly and reasonably competent person, most children will end up enjoying their time with the sitter, even if they do hate to see you go.

I have just discovered that I am expecting another baby. How soon do you think I should break this news to my three-year-old?
Opinions differ on this. Some experts believe that it is better to wait until a month or two before the birth. Tell a young child much sooner than this, they say, and you will run into the difficulty of his limited idea of time.

Having no notion of how long five or six months are, a little child is likely to keep on asking, "Is the baby coming today?" On the other hand, we have to bear in mind that even the youngest children are remarkably observant. They are quick to note changes in their mother. They also pick up ideas from overhearing adult conversations. Once they sense that something is going on, they will put their own interpretation on it. For this reason, it may be wiser to tell your child about the baby as soon as it becomes obvious that you are pregnant, and the coming baby is being discussed with family or friends. That way, the child will have a chance to ask questions, and gain reassurance from his parents, rather than trying to figure things out—probably wrongly—for himself.

What should I tell my child about the new baby?
The wisest approach is to tell your child simply and truthfully that "we are going to have a new baby in our family." Remember that, whatever happens, your older child is going to be jealous of the new arrival. It will not help to tell him that it is because you love him so much that you have decided to have another baby "just like him." As far as he is concerned, if you love him that much, you would not want another child. Nor is it a good idea to pretend that the new arrival will be a playmate for your child, or will be "his baby, too." He will find out soon enough that a tiny baby is not a suitable playmate for a three-year-old.

You might take him visiting where there is a baby, so that he gets a realistic idea of what a baby will be like. You could show him picture books about babies, and let him help you shop for items for the new baby—remembering to include some purchases for him, too. Be prepared for questions about where the baby is coming from, and remember to point out that you do not know whether it will be a boy or a girl. It is very important to avoid any major changes in your three-year-old's life around the time the baby is due—going to nursery school or changing bedrooms, for example—and to give him as much time and attention as usual. Of course, you should still expect your child to be jealous when the new baby finally arrives, and you will want to ensure that he gets plenty of extra attention. Let him help with the baby as much as he wants to, but don't force his interest, or scold him for signs of ill feeling. Above all, let him know over and over again how much you love him.

How can parents tell a young child about the death of someone close to him?

Unless there are some special reasons to the contrary, a child should be told as soon as possible of the death of a beloved relative, a close friend, or even a pet. Keeping the death a secret can only make it harder to explain later. Experts suggest that the best approach is to say simply that the person has died, and will not come back. Say that everyone is very sad because he died, and will miss him very much. Just as an adult needs to work through his feelings of grief, a child also needs to take part in family expressions of sorrow, and to share recollections about the dead person. It can also comfort the child to be told that the person who died will no longer endure sickness and suffering. It is important, however, to make sure that the child doesn't get the impression that people who go into the hospital never come out. Explanations of death as "a long, long sleep" should also be avoided. Children who are told this can become terrified of going to sleep. Whatever further explanations you give will depend to a large extent on your child's reaction, and the kind of questions he asks; but remember that, whatever you tell your child, it is your manner as you talk to him, and your reassurances, that will count as much as what you say.

What can I say to reassure a child who asks when will I die, and who is obviously anxious about dying himself?

A child's major concern when first confronting death is likely to be about the possibility of his parents dying and leaving him, and reassurance on this point is very important. Some people believe that this is one time when a "little white lie" is permissible, and tell their child that they will always be there, and will never leave him. Others prefer to stick more closely to the truth and say, "I won't die for a long, long, long, long time." This is better than saying that people only die when they are very old, because as far as a young child is concerned, "old" can apply to anyone over the age of 20, and certainly to his parents. To questions about a child's own death, you could also stress that he will not die for a very, very, very long time.

How can I answer a child who asks, "What happens when you die?" and "Where do people go when they die"?

In describing death itself, you could explain that when a person, or animal, dies, "his body stops working and can't be fixed again," so that the child won't wonder about his coming back. For a child with a religious background, it can be comforting to be told that the person has gone to live with God, or in heaven. Care should be taken, however, in answering questions about where heaven is. One child who had located heaven in the sky, for example, begged his mother to take him up in an airplane to be near Grandma. Another child became frightened at the idea of dead people watching her from above. Parents who have no religious beliefs may say they just don't know, or that no one knows. Some think that, since a young child needs reassurance, it can help to say that some people believe there is a nice place called heaven where people go when they die. Others prefer to say simply that the dead person's body is buried in a nice cemetery. But here again, it is important to ensure that the child does not get frightening ideas about a living person being buried under the ground, or burned. One explanation you may find helpful is to stress that death is a natural event. Just as flowers and leaves die, so do people, although humans live longer.

133

Sex and the Young Child

When does a child usually begin to masturbate?

Probably as soon as he discovers the pleasurable sensations that come from touching his sexual organs. Just as a young baby plays with his toes, or pulls at his ears, he also begins to explore his genitals. This is a period of finding out about himself—about the good feelings that come from his arms and legs, his feet and hands, and his genitals. When young children masturbate, they are simply exercising their curiosity, and experimenting with the ways of producing pleasurable feelings. Masturbating gives them one kind of pleasure, playing with toys another, being held by their parents another. This is a normal phase of a child's development, generally occurring during infancy, and again between the ages of three and five.

How should I react when my child masturbates?

Fortunately, few parents today believe that masturbation causes mental illness, sterility, or other dire consequences. But we may still feel uncomfortable about it. Even the most open-minded parents, anxious to avoid making their child feel guilty or ashamed about this activity, may wonder how they should react to it. Certainly it is important not to appear shocked or disapproving. The best solution of all is simply to ignore it.

That may work at home, but what can I do if my child masturbates in public?

Try to divert his attention to other things. Most small children are easily distracted when presented with another activity. Rather than pulling his hand away, try handing him one of his toys, and he will probably refocus his attention. If he doesn't, then it is time to say, "You know, there are some things we do only in private, at home, so wait till we get home to do that."

What if my child masturbates a great deal? Shouldn't I then try to stop it? How can I best do so?

Parents would be wise to react if their child masturbates very frequently or excessively, for this behavior is likely to be a symptom of some other problem in the child's life. The child who masturbates excessively is a troubled child, and parents will probably notice other indications of distress, too. Maybe he is not getting enough attention or comfort. Perhaps he needs more holding, and reassurance that he is loved. When a child gets enough affection, and has plenty of satisfying activities to hold his interest, he will be much less likely to go on seeking stimulation and comfort through masturbation. It is important not to scold or shame your child about this behavior, but you could let him know that you are aware of what he is doing, and, while you know it feels good, you would prefer that he did not do it so often.

I recently found my four-year-old

daughter "playing doctor" with the little boy from next door. Both children had their pants down, and were obviously examining each other. Is it best not to interfere, as my neighbor thinks, or am I right to be concerned?

Almost all children do, at some time, "play doctor," or engage in other forms of sex play. This is a natural result of their curiosity about each other's bodies, and about their own physical feelings. For this reason, some child specialists recommend that parents regard such exploration in much the same way as occasional masturbation, accepting it as normal behavior, and only trying to discourage it if it seems excessive. Others— and that includes many mothers—feel that limits should be set on such activities, but wonder how to do this without harming their child's positive feelings about sex. Certainly it would be unwise to scold, spank, or punish your child for indulging in sex play. There is no need to pounce on the children, and demand what they are doing, or tell them that they are being naughty. Instead, you could simply suggest that they get dressed, and find something else to play with. The important thing is your attitude. If you appear shocked or horrified, you are likely to convey the impression that sexual activity is wrong or shameful. If, on the other hand, you remain calm and casual, you can still let the children know that "undressing is not allowed." Answering your child's questions about the differences between boys and girls may also help.

What should I tell my child about sexually abnormal people? How can I warn him against strangers without taking away his trust in adults, or frightening him unnecessarily?

This is a big worry for all parents. Everyone agrees that children must be warned of possible dangers from sex offenders, but opinions differ on how this should be handled. With a young child, the best approach is probably to explain that, while most people are kind and friendly, some are not. You could say that there are people who sometimes try to take children away from their parents, and who might even hurt them. For this reason, tell your child he should never go anywhere with strangers unless Mommy or Daddy tell him to, and he should never accept presents from strangers, or take rides from anyone unless you know about it. This, in addition to your own vigilance, will probably be sufficient to protect your child without alarming him unduly. More specific information, some experts feel, would be of little practical help, and might frighten a child unnecessarily. Others disagree. They consider that if, in addition to your warnings, a child is given some idea of the nature of the danger, he will be better equipped to cope with any unpleasant incident that might occur. They suggest parents explain that some people are "sort of sick" on account of bad things that have happened to them, and that these people may sometimes show their genitals to other people, or like to undress young children and play with them. Provided you are careful to present this information objectively, stressing an understanding of such people rather than overemphasizing the dangers, experts think that you can arm your child with knowledge without making him unduly fearful. Only you can decide which attitude to adopt, and how much to tell your child. There is, however, one important point in favor of giving a child some information about sexually disturbed adults. Such people are not always strangers. Unfortunately, unpleasant experiences sometimes involve a person the child knows. Looking back on her own childhood, one woman reports how her mother's words helped her to handle such an encounter. "If you ever feel uncomfortable about someone touching you," her mother said, "if you feel that there is something wrong about it, and you want to run away, then your feelings are right and you must obey them, even if you are with someone you, Mommy, and Daddy all know, and you need never be afraid to tell us about it."

Solving Family Arguments

Breakfast time is chaos in our house. No matter how I nag, threaten, or plead, getting our nine-year-old daughter up and off to school on time is a daily battle. What can I do?

Few of us feel bright and alert first thing in the morning, and the breakfast rush can make the best run home seem like a madhouse. Children tend to rebel against adult schedules, and the more you urge them to hurry, the more they dawdle. So what can you do? First, accept that your daughter finds it hard to get out of bed in the morning, and that she is not going to respond to nagging. Telling her how lazy she is, shouting at her, trying soft persuasion will not help. Instead, call her in plenty of time, make sure she is awake, and then leave it up to her.

Secondly, don't insist she sit down to eat breakfast if she doesn't want to. Rather, put out some fruit juice, milk, toast and butter, cheese, hard-boiled egg, or apples that she can eat quickly, or even take with her to eat on the way. Getting books and lunch money together the night before, or leaving her lunch box by the door will also be more helpful than last-minute lectures about forgetfulness. Don't coax, push, or tell your daughter to hurry. Simply let her know, "It's 8 o'clock," or, "The school bus will be here in 10 minutes." Remember, she is the one who will be in trouble if she is late to school, not you. If you let her know that you regard this as her responsibility, she is far more likely to try to be on time.

It's all very well to say we should listen to our children, but how do we get them to listen to us? My son is always complaining that he "forgot" what I said or "didn't hear" when I called him.

Most parents could give examples of this "temporary deafness" on the part of their children. A schoolage child tends to become engrossed in what he is doing, and may often seem to tune his parents out when they are talking about subjects he doesn't consider important, or issuing commands he would rather not hear. Getting your child to listen, then, may be first and foremost a matter of capturing his attention before you speak. Call him, and wait for him to respond by looking up from his book or game, or answering "Yes," before you ask him to do something. Giving him this opportunity to refocus his attention will save more time and temper than endless reminders of requests that went unheard. Try also to give fewer instructions—stick to the ones that are essential, and that he will have time to carry through. Children soon grow wise to the number of times parents will repeat an order before attempting to enforce it. Keep instructions simple, especially for a younger child. Avoid lengthy explanations. "What did you say?" or "But what I want to know is . . ." can be a child's signal that we have wandered from the point. There may, however, be times when your child does need to hear the same information over and over again. Explanations of sex, death, or the absence of a parent might have to be repeated patiently and often, but they should still be kept as uncomplicated as possible. If we try to use words meaningfully—to express our feelings, to reassure and inform more often than to scold or criticize—and if we are willing listeners ourselves, our children will be more inclined to pay attention most of the time.

Have you any suggestions on persuading an untidy teenager to straighten up his room?

A teenager's room is his domain. Any suggestion that he keep it tidy—or even clean—is likely to be met with, "It's *my* room, and I like it this way." So, while parents can insist that dirty clothes or decaying apple cores are unhealthy, it may be wiser to come to a compromise over the rest of the clutter that most teenagers seem to enjoy. Calling your teenager sloppy or messy isn't helpful. Better to limit discussion to the problem in hand, and look for a solution you can both live with. How much would it matter if your teenager only cleaned his room once or twice a month instead of every week, provided he makes his bed and empties the wastebasket regularly? In the meantime, could you keep his door closed, and just leave the room as it is?

What about getting teenagers to do their share of household chores?

Where tasks affecting the whole family are concerned, parents can be firmer about expecting some help. The first step is to involve your children in making rules about work around the house. What needs to be done, and who will take responsibility for what? It helps if children can see that tasks are shared fairly by all the family, parents included. Rather than always doing the dishes or setting the table, can Jane have a chance to cook a meal, or plan the week's menus? Instead of always being the one to take out the garbage or mow the lawn, can Joe prepare his own food for a picnic, or pick up the groceries from the supermarket? Some families find that the best way to get over the most boring jobs is to do them together. A major cleanup every Saturday morning, for example, with everyone helping, may save time and squabbles. Of course, children, like any of us, will take more kindly to doing a job they like than one they hate. You'll get more cooperation if you give him some choice about when to do a particular chore, not waiting until the last minute before asking him to wash the car, or interrupting his homework with a request for help. Of course, he won't always do a perfect job, but nagging and criticizing will only make him feel less like helping next time. Letting him know when his help has made life easier for us, on the other hand, can make even the dullest chore seem more worthwhile.

Whenever I talk to my teenager about keeping the house tidy, he says, "What for"? How do you answer that one?

A lot of controversy over chores arises because youngsters don't see why many of them need to be done at all. As far as they are concerned, a trail of wet towels in the bathroom, or a litter of records and empty cans about the place may be perfectly acceptable. So let's say frankly that we simply want to make home comfortable and pleasant for everyone, so that we can all enjoy living there. We can freely admit how tedious certain tasks are, but emphasize the positive aspects of getting them done. "Good—now I'll have time to catch that TV program," can tell your youngster that his help was needed and appreciated. Maybe your teenager will say, "The house doesn't need to be *that* clean—you're too fussy." Well, are you? Sometimes we go overboard for orderliness at the cost of comfort and family harmony. Are there some tasks that need not be done so often, or so thoroughly? Ask your family for their ideas. Could you help Bob turn his room into a den/bedroom so that he and his friends don't have to mess up the living room? How much would it matter if Sam left the dishes for a couple of hours instead of doing them right after dinner? On the other hand, you shouldn't hesitate to express your needs, too. "It really bugs me to have to clear up a load of empty cans and potato chip bags before I can sit down in comfort," or "It makes me furious to see the kitchen in a mess when I worked so hard to get it clean," can be more effective than hours of nagging.

How should parents react when agreed chores don't get done?

The best approach, if you can manage it, is to say something like, "Hey, I thought we agreed that you would do the dishes this evening." That's more helpful than snapping, "Can't you do what you promised?" Better to say, "I'm disappointed you didn't keep our bargain," than to rage, "I pity the girl who marries you!" Showing our youngster that we expect, and trust, him to keep to his commitments—and giving him a chance to explain when he doesn't—can be the surest way to encourage cooperation as well as communication.

Whatever I say to my son seems to be wrong. How can a mother be sympathetic toward her teenager when she's the one who's under attack?

The answer is that she can't—at least not always. No one can be kind and understanding all the time, and in any family there has to be room for parents' moods and feelings as well as their children's. When your teenager is irritable and snappy, and seems to turn on you for no reason at all, it can be hard indeed to keep your temper. If your child has really made you angry, or you are feeling tired and upset yourself, it is best to say so. A teenager can easily feel guilty if allowed to go too far, and if you can stop an argument firmly before it becomes a pitched battle, so much the better. Sometimes you may be able to ignore the literal content of your teenager's attack— "You always think you know everything," "You never stop nagging," "You make me sick!"—as the gross exaggeration it is. Other times, your calmness may merely provoke a more outspoken attempt to raise a reaction. Whatever the case, however, it is important to try to avoid matching your teenager's attacks with equally bitter generalizations of your own. Sweeping condemnations of his lack of respect, or attacks on his personality, appearance, or abilities, will simply drive you further apart. Of course, it's hard not to do this. We may know perfectly well that it is normal for adolescents to criticize their parents, but when it is *our* child finding fault with *us*, things look different. We should, however, try to remind ourselves that our child's criticisms are not evidence of our failure as parents, or proof that he no longer loves us.

Our 16-year-old daughter has an 11:30 p.m. curfew, but she is nearly always late. I can't sleep until she's home, and we always end up having a fight. How can you get a teenager to respect agreements about homecoming hours?

When your daughter is late, you worry. So the best policy may be to tell her so. How about saying, "Look, I trust you to try to get home by the time we agreed. I don't want to spoil your evening by nagging. But if you are delayed, I get worried sick that you might have been in an accident or something. So if you're going to be late for some reason, call. Then we can both have a good time." Of course, if your daughter doesn't keep to the agreement, you should tell her frankly that you're upset. But rather than translating your anxiety into rage, try telling her first how relieved you are that she is home safe. If you let her know that it is because you love her so much that you are concerned, she will be less apt to feel that you are simply out to keep her from enjoying herself. You may find it helpful to show your daughter that you are willing to extend her curfew by half-an-hour or so sometimes, according to the occasion. But once you have agreed on a homecoming time, you will have to remain firm.

138

Sex and Your Teenager

Our 12-year-old is miserable because she is not maturing physically as fast as her friends. Is there anything we can say to comfort her?

Life can be hard for the young adolescent who finds herself temporarily "left behind" by friends of the same age—and just when it is so important to be like everyone else. The early bloomer, too, is likely to feel awkward and self-conscious, but it is often the late developer who suffers most, not only feeling left out, but maybe also secretly worrying that something is wrong with her. That is why it is important to reassure your daughter that variations in the rate of growth are perfectly normal. If you, or other members of your family, were also late developers, it may help to point this out. Sometimes developing a particular skill or hobby can boost the self-esteem of a slow grower, especially if it involves activities with people of varying ages. Comforting your daughter probably won't be easy. Patience is a virtue in short supply at age 12, and, of course, parents cannot do the one thing their child wants most—speed up her development. But you can give her the support she needs to wait out this difficult phase.

What attitude should parents take toward masturbation during adolescence?

Masturbation is a natural outlet for the buildup of sexual tension in adolescence, a temporary way of coping with new and intense sexual feelings. Nevertheless, most teenagers will feel self-conscious about it, and most parents will probably find it hard to discuss the subject openly with their children.

It is important, however, to avoid giving a teenager the impression that masturbation is harmful, or that the sexual daydreams that may accompany it are shameful and wrong. It may be possible when talking to a teenager about sex, for example, to say that sexual feelings can be hard to handle when you're in your teens, that many boys and girls masturbate sometimes, and that this does not hurt them in any way, or make them less capable of enjoying sex later on. The best approach from parents is one of casual reassurance that does not draw too much embarrassing attention to what is, after all, a very private affair. Of course, masturbation can become excessive but, as in the case of the younger child, this is a signal that something else is going wrong in a youngster's life, and it is the cause of his behavior that parents should look for, rather than directing their concern only toward the behavior itself.

What should parents tell their teenager about birth control?

Many parents worry about when and how—and even if—they should give their children information about contraception. They fear that talking about such matters to a young teenager may upset him, stimulate his curiosity, or encourage him toward sexual experimentation. However, it would be a

139

mistake to believe that if the subject is not mentioned, a child is not going to be concerned about it. Even an 11- or 12-year-old will be picking up bits of information, or misinformation, from other sources. It would seem far wiser, then, for parents to provide him with helpful knowledge about contraception. It is the opinion of many psychiatrists that this information is best given, along with other facts about sex, before a child is himself involved in making decisions about it. Knowing how to prevent pregnancy, they argue, is unlikely to encourage an emotionally healthy teenager to become promiscuous. Of course, teenagers need to know about methods that are unreliable—using homemade improvisations, counting on the so-called "safe-period," practicing withdrawal, and so on—as well as those that are effective. Teenagers should also be informed about where they can get further information about contraception if they wish.

With today's changing attitudes toward morality, what can parents tell their teenager about premarital sex, and the dangers of promiscuity? I am afraid my attitude would be regarded as rather old-fashioned, so how can I make my standards sound reasonable to my teenager?

The teenager today is faced with a bewildering paradox when it comes to establishing desirable standards of sexual behavior. On the one hand, he lives in a society in which sexual stimulation for profit is openly exploited in advertising and entertainment. On the other, he is told that society does not approve of teenagers seeking sexual fulfillment before marriage. Small wonder, then, that the teenager is confused, and that he should accuse the adult world of hypocrisy. That is why it is so important for parents to think through their own standards—whatever these may be—and to make them clear to their teenager. You owe it to your teenager, and yourself, to tell him or her how you feel and why. Teenagers want guidance, and it would be a mistake not to offer that guidance out of a fear of appearing old-fashioned. If you believe that true sexual fulfillment can only come within the framework of a long-term relationship between two people who love, respect, and are committed to each other, say so. If you feel that a sexual relationship should carry with it a sense of responsibility toward the other person, a concern for that person's good, and an unwillingness to hurt or pressure him or her, say that, too. It is not enough to tell a teenager that sex before marriage "is wrong," or to warn of the dangers of unwanted pregnancy or venereal disease. But we can talk to him, or her, about sexual values within the whole context of human relationships. Exactly what you say to your teenager must, of course, depend on your own views, and he will have to decide for himself whether or not to accept your guidance. But the youngster whose self-esteem is high, and who has seen within his own home the example of a loving and caring relationship, is far more likely to seek the same kind of responsible relationship for himself.

Supposing your daughter says, "Several girls I know are taking the pill. Don't you think I should?" How would you answer.

From time to time many teenagers will drop remarks like this, as a kind of feeler to test their parents' reaction. The answer is that we need to look beyond the question itself, and try to find out what our youngster really wants to know. Is she asking us to take the responsibility for deciding whether or not she should experiment with sex? Is she looking for our support in resisting pressure to behave as some of her friends are doing? Is she seriously considering an involvement, and wanting to be responsible about it? Certainly parents can point out that decisions about sex should be based on her own individual feelings of what is right for her, and not on what her friends are doing. However, if parents know that their daughter is planning to have sexual relations, they would be unwise to stop her from obtaining professional advice about contraception, especially if this could include some counseling about teenage relationships as well.

What can a parent say to a teenage son or daughter who maintains, "Everyone looks down on you if you are inexperienced"?

First of all we can sympathize with our teenager's dilemma. We can say that we know how difficult it can be to take one's own individual stand on sexual behavior, particularly when sexual feelings are strong, when we are curious to learn more about what sex is like, and when we want to be attractive and popular with others. But we can emphasize that he has the power of choice in this, as in other decisions about how he wants to live his life, and that each person's respect for himself depends on being true to his own feelings and convictions, and no one else's. We can say that there is no reason to feel abnormal if he does not feel he should have sexual relations, or if he doesn't want to make a decision yet. Different people have different needs and standards of behavior, and each of us must do what we feel to be the right thing for us. We can point out, too, that people are not always as experienced as they like to appear, but that it is far more important and worthwhile to be honest with ourselves than to abandon our principles for the sake of superficial popularity.

My daughter complains that when she refused sex, her boyfriend didn't ask her out again, and started dating another girl who is an easy mark. What can I say to her?

Start by telling your daughter that she made a wise decision in not agreeing to something she did not feel right about. It is only natural that a boy who finds her attractive should want to make a pass, but if he is seriously interested in her as a person, he will not reject her for refusing. In fact, he may well admire her a great deal more for having the courage of her convictions, and if he genuinely likes her, he will want to stay around. The boy who is only looking for sexual release may seek out the easy mark, but he is unlikely to be interested in building a deeper relationship with her. When your daughter meets a boy who is drawn to her emotionally as well as physically, he will be willing to wait until she is ready for an intimate involvement.

I feel terribly uncomfortable about discussing sex at all with my teenager. How can I get over this difficulty?

Take heart. Very few parents would say they found this easy, for no matter how much more openly we may talk about sex these days, there are still certain natural taboos within a family that make it a hard subject for discussion between parents and teenager. Many of us will ourselves have been raised in families that did not discuss sex, so we may be breaking new ground as well as trying to prepare our teenagers for life in a more permissive age. Perhaps the best way to get around this embarrassment is to be honest about it. We can tell our teenager, "Look, I wish I felt more comfortable about discussing this with you. People were much less frank about these things when I was growing up, and that makes it harder for me to talk to you now. But I do think it's important to try. So can you bear with me if I get a bit flustered? At least you shouldn't have the same trouble with your children!" We've already mentioned how useful books on sex education for teenagers can be in helping you to collect your thoughts, and present your ideas more easily. In some cases, of course, parents will prefer to let their teenager have a book that they consider appropriate. If you know that you will never be able to discuss the subject sufficiently comfortably, try to find someone who can: a relative or family friend, a doctor, school counselor, youth leader, or minister. But try to make sure that the person you choose really has an understanding and positive attitude toward both sex, and the particular problems of teenagers.

141

Talking About Drugs

How can I ensure that my teenager doesn't experiment with drugs?

The answer is that you can't. Every teenager is going to have to judge for himself at some point whether or not he should try drugs, and we cannot make that decision for him. What we can do is to ensure that our teenager has the kind of information and guidance on which to base a sensible attitude of his own toward drug taking.

What kind of information should I be giving my teenager about drugs?

Questions about drugs, like those about sex, will not arise suddenly one day to be dealt with in a single, straightforward answer. This is a topic that is likely to crop up again and again over the years, probably from the time your teenager is still quite young, and we must be fully aware of the facts about drugs ourselves, so that we can answer our youngster's questions as they arise. After all, if we make incorrect statements, he is not likely to pay much attention to our guidance on the subject. If we simply issue a blanket warning about the horrifying dangers of all drugs, for example, what will be the reaction of a youngster who sees one of his friends happily smoking marijuana without apparent harm? We need to be ready to discuss the differences between various drugs, and to talk about why people use them as well as the risks involved. As we answer our teenager's questions, we will, of course, also be letting him know how we feel about drug use, and how we hope he will act. But we should be prepared for the fact that even a teenager who has never tried drugs may hotly defend the right of his peers to do so. Your teenager may tell you that he has tried marijuana once or twice, at the urging of friends, or out of sheer curiosity. Don't panic or react defensively, but try to remember how many of us sampled a drink or a cigarette in our teens for the very same reasons. In any discussion about drugs it is important to let our teenager have his say, and be prepared to talk over his arguments. It is this kind of open discussion with parents who are obviously speaking from a knowledge of the facts that will impress a teenager far more than condemnations and warnings.

"What's wrong with smoking grass?" says our teenager. "It's no worse than alcohol. In fact, it is *less* dangerous." How do you answer that one?

"Yes," we can say, "on present evidence it certainly seems that marijuana is much less harmful than other drugs, including alcohol —and tobacco for that matter. But that doesn't mean that marijuana is *harmless*." We could go on to say that research is still continuing into the long-term effects of even moderate use of marijuana. In the meantime, we know that, for some people, marijuana can become the major focus of interest in life, offering an easy escape from their problems, and causing them to lose interest in other aims and activities. This can become more of a danger during the teenage years, when a young person may already be finding life difficult and confusing. He may find it harder to concentrate on studying or other activities, or to get back to handling his life constructively once he has sought an easy way out. We can point out that marijuana affects different people different ways—and at different times. Although effects like altered perception of time and distance, or lapse of memory, do, of course, wear off, some people have experienced severe reactions to marijuana. This may have been due to contamination of the drug with another substance—and that, too, is a risk so long as marijuana remains illegal. The fact that marijuana is illegal is an important point to make to your teenager when comparing it with alcohol. In many states, the penalties for use, or even possession, are extremely severe. Young people are being sent to jail for marijuana offenses. Is this a risk that your youngster wants to take?

What if your teenager replies, "Well, the law is wrong. It should be changed"?

We may agree with our teenager that the present laws are too harsh. But we can point out that, even if marijuana were legalized, its sale would almost certainly be restricted to those over the age of 18, just as the age for driving a car or drinking in a bar are controlled. In the meantime, we could say that we would like him to put off any decision about using marijuana, or alcohol, until he is, say, at least 18.

My son has suggested I try marijuana, arguing that, "You can't know what you're talking about if you've never tried it." Should I do so?

No. You may feel that your son has the right to decide whether or not *he* should try marijuana, but that doesn't mean you should put yourself in the position of giving him permission to do so. If you are trying to give your teenager positive reasons for not using drugs, accepting his challenge could seriously undermine your arguments. Instead, you might say that much of our knowledge about many things is drawn from observation, from the evidence of other people's experience, and from the facts of scientific research. We do not have to have personal experience of the risks involved in certain behavior before deciding how we should act. This reasoning may not satisfy your son, but it is best to avoid being drawn into a full-scale argument on this one point.

Our teenager accuses us of being hypocritical about marijuana. "You smoke and drink, and so do your friends," he says, "So why shouldn't I use pot?" What can we say?

Many of us feel justified in replying, a little crossly perhaps, that it is not logical for our teenager to criticize our use of cigarettes or alcohol on the one hand, and then use something that is a substitute for cigarettes or alcohol to him. Others might simply say that cigarettes and alcohol are legal, and pot is not. But this is not enough. If we want our children to understand the risks involved in using any drug, including alcohol and tobacco, we have to be more constructive. We shouldn't be afraid to admit that we, and other adults, do not always act in our own best interests. Where cigarettes are concerned, we may say that we began smoking before the health risks were so well known, and that it is now very hard for us to stop. If we are making serious efforts to quit smoking, of course, our argument will carry more weight. Alcohol, too, has been a socially acceptable part of adult life ever since we grew up. We should be frank with our children about the dangers of alcohol, and let them know that we disapprove of the excessive use of this or any drugs by anybody, including ourselves. But provided we drink occasionally and in moderation, we need not feel that this will be a disastrous example for our children. The important thing is to be honest with our teenager, and to show him that we are willing to look objectively at *our* use of drugs as well as *his*.

For Your Bookshelf

Infants and Mothers
by T. Berry Brazelton, M.D., Delacorte Press (New York: 1969); Hutchinson & Co. Ltd. (London: 1972)

Your Child's Self-Esteem: The Key to His Life
by Dorothy Corkille Briggs, Doubleday & Co., Inc. (New York: 1970)

The Emerging Personality
Infancy to Adolescence, by George E. Gardner, M.D., Ph.D., Delacorte Press (New York: 1970); Hutchinson & Co. Ltd. (London: 1971)

What Every Child Would Like His Parents to Know
by Dr. Lee Salk, David McKay Co., Inc. (New York: 1972)

What Shall We Tell The Kids?
by Bennett Olshaker, M.D., Arbor House Publishing Co., Inc. (New York: 1971); paperback edition, Dell Publishing Co., Inc. (New York: 1973)

Between Parent and Child: New Solutions to Old Problems
by Dr. Haim G. Ginott, The Macmillan Company (New York: 1965); paperback edition, Avon Books (New York: 1969, 1973); Pan Books Ltd. (London: 1969)

Between Parent and Teenager
by Dr. Haim G. Ginott, The Macmillan Company (New York: 1969); paperback edition, Avon Books (New York: 1971, 1973)

Growing into Adolescence
A Sensible Guide for Parents of Children 11 to 14, by Lynn Minton, Parents' Magazine Press (New York: 1972)

Natural Parenthood: Raising Your Child without a Script
by Eda J. LeShan, Signet Books (New York: 1970)

You, Your Child and Drugs
by the staff of the Child Study Association of America, The Child Study Press (New York: 1971)

Picture Credits